QUANTIFY YOUR IMPACT

QUANTIFY YOUR IMPACT

How to Turn Everyday Work into Measurable Business Impact

PETER B. NICHOL

For information about permissions to reproduce selections from the book, or about special discounts for bulk purchases, please contact: booksales@datasciencecio.com

First Edition

Publisher's Catalog-in-Publication Data
Library of Congress Catalog Card LCCN No. 2026902674

ISBN: 978-1-7363859-2-0

Printed in the United States of America.

To every leader tired of explaining their value.
You no longer have to. Walk with me.

CONTACTING PETER B. NICHOL

Everything can be quantified—especially the work that too often goes unseen.

What I've learned is this: Most professionals are confident they're creating value, but far fewer can prove it in the moments that matter. In rooms where priorities are set, budgets are approved, and strategies are reshaped, effort alone is invisible. Business leaders, business relationship managers, product owners, product managers, project managers, and IT leaders all feel the weight of this reality. Their teams are doing meaningful work every day, yet when asked to explain that work in terms that drive decisions, the story often falls apart. Not because the value isn't there but because the work lives in the gray—outside of neat metrics, tidy dashboards, and simplistic scorecards. And it's in that gray space where impact is most often discounted, misunderstood, or lost entirely.

Since becoming the first globally certified Master Business Relationship Manager through the BRM Institute in 2019, and through the creation and delivery of the BRM Accelerator Program—Phase One, *Mindset over Mechanics*, and Phase Two, *Practice over Theory*—I've seen this challenge surface repeatedly at the executive level. Leaders often recognize that they are working hard and that their teams are contributing, yet they struggle to translate that effort into language that resonates with senior leadership. Saying a team "did a lot of work last quarter" no longer carries weight. What matters is the ability to explain how that work moved the needle by reducing time, avoiding cost, mitigating risk, increasing capacity, or enabling better decisions.

The intent of this book is to address that gap. *Quantify Your Impact* is designed to provide a simple, repeatable framework that individuals and teams can apply to clearly articulate and quantify the business impact of their work. This is not about theory or abstract models. It is about producing defensible, business-relevant measures that leaders can understand, trust, and act upon.

I also welcome your stories, insights, and any useful tools or techniques you've discovered that improve how ideas are formed and how work is delivered with excellence. I guarantee that I'll read every letter and email I receive; however, due to volume, I'm not able to respond personally to every request for information.

For leaders, teams, and organizations interested in engaging me for board advisory, consulting, or speaking, please contact me at OROCA Innovations:

Peter B. Nichol
Chief Technology Officer, OROCA Innovations
14201 Arrow Point Ct

Estero, FL 33829
E-mail: peter.nichol@datasciencecio.com
Twitter: @peterbnichol

For additional information on the book, *Deliver Real Value*, please visit the website:
www.datasciencecio.com/deliverrealvalue

For additional information on the book, *Earn Strategic Trust*, please visit the website:
www.datasciencecio.com/earnstrategictrust

For additional information on the book, *Quantify Your Impact*, please visit the website:
www.datasciencecio.com/quantifyyourimpact

For additional information on the book, *Leading With Value*, please visit the website:
www.datasciencecio.com/leadingwithvalue

For additional information on the book, *Think Lead Disrupt*, please visit the website: www.datasciencecio.com/thinkleaddisrupt

For additional information on the book, *The Power of Block-chain for Healthcare*, please visit the website: www.datasciencecio.com/blockchainbook

For additional information on the book, *Learning Intelligence*, please visit the website: www.datasciencecio.com/li

ABOUT THE AUTHOR

PETER B. NICHOL (@peterbnichol) is a technology executive with 25 years of experience who's dedicated to driving innovation, digital transformation, leadership, and data in business. He helps organizations connect strategy to execution to maximize company performance.

Peter has led businesses through complex changes including the adoption of data-first approaches for portfolio management, Lean Six Sigma for operational excellence, departmental transformations, process improvements, maximizing team performance, designing new IT operating models, digitizing platforms, leading large-scale mission-critical technology deployments, product management, agile methodologies, and building high-performance teams.

Peter has been recognized for Digital Innovation by CIO 100, MIT Sloan, Computerworld, BRM Institute, and the Project Management Institute. As Managing Director at OROCA Innovations, Peter leads the CXO advisory-services practice that drives digital strategies.

Peter was honored as an MIT Sloan CIO Leadership Award Finalist in 2015 and is a regular contributor to CIO.com on innovation. As Head of Information Technology, Peter was responsible for Connecticut's Health Insurance Exchange's (HIX) industry-leading digital platform, which has transformed consumerism and retail-oriented services for the health-insurance industry. Peter championed the Connecticut marketplace digital implementation with a transformational, cloud-based, SaaS platform and mobile application. He was recognized as a 2014 PMI Project of the Year Award finalist, CIO 100, and received awards for best digital services, API, and platform. He also received a lifetime achievement award for leadership and digital transformation and was honored as a 2016 Computerworld Premier 100 IT Leader.

Peter has a Bachelor of Science in Computer Information Systems from Bentley University and a Master in Business

Administration from Quinnipiac University, where he graduated Summa Cum Laude. He earned his PMP® in 2001 and is a certified Six Sigma Master Black Belt, Certified SAFe® Lean Portfolio Manager, Certified SAFe® Agilist, Certified SAFe® Practitioner (SP), Certified ScrumMaster®, Business Relationship Management Professional (BRMP®), Certified Business Relationship Manager (CBRM®), and the first globally credentialled Master of Business Relationship Management (MBRM®) by the BRM Institute. Together we can change the world!

For more details, please visit www.datasciencecio.com/about/

ACCLAIM FOR THE BOOK

"*Quantify Your Impact* is a book for professionals who want to be evaluated on results, not activity. It offers a practical method for expressing contributions with precision and restraint—qualities leaders tend to trust."

— RAMESH NATARAJAN
HEAD OF GENAI AND MACHINE LEARNING SOLITIONS, DANIICHI SANKYO US

"Most organizations reward activity because impact is harder to see. *Quantify Your Impact* shows professionals how to close that gap by expressing their work in terms leaders can evaluate—time, cost, risk, and capacity. This book replaces ambiguity with clarity."

— JEN RAUTMANN
IT DIRECTOR, BRM AND BUSINESS ALIGNMENT, NAVICO GROUP

"Ideas don't change businesses—leaders who know how to execute them do. Nichol connects innovation, leadership, and measurable outcomes in a way that is both practical and provocative. *Quantify Your Impact* is a compelling read for anyone responsible for turning ambition into results."

— MATT WEBB
SENIOR DIRECTOR, ENTERPRISE BUSINESS PROCESS(IT), BRUNSWICK CORPORATION

"Rarely does a business book speak equally well to senior leaders and frontline managers. Nichol bridges that gap by showing exactly how strategic value is created, measured, and communicated at every level. *Quantify Your Impact* is the playbook leaders have been missing!"

— MICHAEL FLANARY
IT BUSINESS RELATIONSHIP MANAGER,
MOFFITT CANCER CENTER

"Most professionals know they create value—but can't prove it. *Quantify Your Impact* closes that gap. Nichol gives readers a clear, defensible way to translate everyday work into the metrics leaders actually use to make decisions. This book turns contribution into credibility!"

— BHAWESH CHOUDHARY
DIRECTOR, ROBOTIC PROCESS AUTOMATION & ENTERPRISE INTEGRATION, REGENERON

"Whether you're preparing for a performance review, a promotion, or your next role, *Quantify Your Impact* teaches you how to tell your story in the language leaders understand. Nichol bridges the gap between hard work and hard numbers, giving professionals a powerful edge at every stage of their career!"

— MARC IPPOLITO
DIRECTOR, CLINICAL PROCESS COMPLIANCE, MANAGEMENT, ABBVIE

ACCLAIM FOR OTHER BOOKS BY PETER B. NICHOL

"After 62, I wasn't ready to give up pickleball — I just didn't understand why my shoulder and knees were suddenly talking back to me. Reading *Stay Strong After 60* gave me clarity I didn't realize I was missing. Instead of pushing through pain, I adjust, strengthen, and keep playing. It's practical, reassuring, and incredibly empowering."

— LINDA MARTINEZ
PICKLEBALL PLAYER AND PROUD GRANDMOTHER
WHO NEVER MISSES LEAGUE NIGHT
CHARLOTTE, NC

"Most BRMs are trusted operationally yet under-leveraged strategically. *Earn Strategic Trust* explains why. It exposes order-taking as a failure mode, not a steppingstone. The result is a role executives can evaluate, rely on, and prioritize."

— ART CAMPBELL
BUSINESS RELATIONSHIP MANAGER, CORPORATION SERVICES,
MOUNT SINAI HEALTH SYSTEMS

"I've seen capable BRMs plateau—not because they lacked talent, but because their role was never clearly defined. *Deliver Real Value* addresses that directly. It gives practitioners a way to earn authority through results, not proximity—and that distinction matters at the executive level.

— VAUGHAN MERLYN
CO-FOUNDER, BUSINESS RELATIONSHIP
MANAGEMENT INSTITUTE

"Learn how to speak the language of business value! *Leading with Value* is the solution that every business relationship partner has been looking for—the complete guide to effectively communicating business value!"

— GLENN REMORERAS
CHIEF INFORMATION OFFICER, MARK ANTHONY GROUP

"*Think Lead Disrupt* presents unique insights on how innovators continually evolve ideas for digital transformation. Nichol shares the secrets to move from strategy to execution. A must read!"

— AMRESH MATHUR
DIGITAL TRANSFORMATION EXECUTIVE,
SAMSUNG ELECTRONICS AMERICA

"*The Power of Blockchain for Healthcare* is an essential read for any seasoned leader, and with Peter's unique perspectives, it's no wonder he is one of the most influential innovation voices on healthcare innovation. A must read."

— GUILHERME STOCCO
HEAD OF STRATEGY AND INNOVATION AT BANCO ORIGINAL

"*Learning Intelligence* extends the current view of personal maturity by introducing LQ—Learning Quotient a complement to intelligence and emotional intelligence by focusing on our ability to change, grow, and live. A fascinating concept every leader should explore."

— THOMAS WALENTA
BOARD OF DIRECTORS AND FELLOW,
PROJECT MANAGEMENT INSTITUTE

TABLE OF CONTENTS

PREFACE

How do you explain the value of your work? Not what you do. Not your role. Not your title. Your value.

Most professionals assume their impact is obvious. That good work speaks for itself. That results will be noticed. But when promotion cycles arrive, when budgets tighten, when resumes are reviewed, or when leaders ask, "What changed because of this?"—that assumption collapses.

Managers don't promote effort. Executives don't fund intentions. Organizations don't reward potential.

They reward impact that can be explained.

Across every role—individual contributors, managers, technical leads, analysts, operators, architects, and executives—the same struggle shows up in different forms. You're asked to write an annual review and freeze at the word "impact." You update your resume and default to listing responsibilities. You lead initiatives that clearly improve things yet struggle to explain why they mattered. You know the work was important—but you can't quite prove it.

Impact is real. The language for it is not.

To ground this, consider a familiar scenario. You're evaluating two candidates for a role. Both are competent. Both have experience. One resume lists tasks: systems supported, projects delivered, tools used. The other explains outcomes: time reduced, risk avoided, capacity created, costs prevented. Which one feels more senior? More credible? More promotable?

The difference isn't ability. It's quantified impact.

This same dynamic plays out in performance reviews, promotion discussions, and leadership conversations every day. Work that changes the system often disappears because it doesn't come with numbers. Preventative work goes unnoticed because nothing "happened." Enablement work gets minimized because it didn't ship a visible artifact. The irony is that some of the most valuable contributions are the hardest to describe.

Throughout my career—working inside large organizations, leading teams, and supporting executives—the same question keeps surfacing in different forms: What changed because of this work—and why should anyone care?

Most people never learn how to answer that question. Not because they lack impact—but because no one taught them how to translate it. That's what this book is for. Not to help you work harder. But to help you make your impact undeniable.

Quantify Your Impact is the guide most professionals didn't know they needed—but have been missing their entire careers. Through years of working inside complex organizations, building systems, leading teams, and watching good work go unnoticed, I've learned that impact is rarely absent. It's simply unmeasured, untranslated, and undefended.

In this book, I focus on how to make impact visible—clearly, credibly, and repeatedly. Not through slogans or storytelling but through disciplined thinking and practical measurement.

This book is organized into five parts:

Part I, Why Most Work Is Invisible (and How to Fix It), establishes the problem this book exists to solve. We examine why modern organizations reward activity over outcomes, why preventive and enabling work disappears, and how well-intentioned metrics often fail to reflect real contribution. This section reframes the challenge from a personal communication issue to a structural one—and introduces the mindset shift required to move from reporting work to quantifying impact.[1]

Part II, The Quantified Impact Framework™, introduces a simple, repeatable method for translating work into business-relevant value. We walk through how to define before and after states, measure what actually changed, and scale that change responsibly into time, cost, risk, and capacity. This section provides the core logic that underpins the rest of the book.[2]

Part III, The Workbook: Real Examples, Real Numbers, applies the framework to practical, operational scenarios. These chapters walk step-by-step through real-world use cases—process friction, analytics, automation, migrations, governance, and systems work—using realistic assumptions and defensible math. The goal is not inspiration but replication.[3]

Part IV, Advanced and Non-Obvious Value, explores impact that is harder to see but often more important: risk reduction, prevention, optionality, and avoided downstream costs. This section expands value beyond labor savings and shows how to quantify change without overstating certainty or credibility.

Part V, Making This Repeatable in Your Organization, brings everything together. We focus on embedding quantified impact into how work is initiated, delivered, reviewed, and funded—without turning value into bureaucracy. This is about making impact visible by default, not retroactively justified.

Quantify Your Impact will change how you think about your work—and how others see it.

The value is already there. This book shows you how to prove it.

Peter Benton Nichol
Estero, FL

ACKNOWLEDGMENTS

The author gratefully acknowledges the many practitioners and leaders across finance, healthcare, life sciences, technology, energy, retail, and data-driven organizations whose insights and experiences informed this work. Special thanks go to those who apply analytics, measurement, and value discipline to real business problems and whose feedback helped translate concepts into practical, repeatable, and defensible impact. Their willingness to challenge assumptions and share lessons from real-world application strengthened both the rigor and relevance of this book.

"When you can measure what you are speaking about, and express it in numbers, you know something about it."

— LORD KELVIN

PART I

WHY MOST WORK IS INVISIBLE (AND HOW TO FIX IT)

Part I explains the problem this book exists to solve.

Most organizations believe they are value driven. In practice, they are visibility driven. Work that is loud, tangible, or easy to describe gets attention. Work that is preventive, connective, or quietly stabilizing disappears. Not because it lacks impact—but because it lacks language.[1]

This section is about why that invisibility is structural, not personal.

Modern operating models reward activity over outcomes, delivery over impact, and motion over change. Teams ship dashboards that don't alter decisions. They automate steps without reclaiming capacity. They absorb risk, reduce friction, and keep systems running—then struggle to explain why any of that matters when budgets tighten.

The result is an impact gap: Real value is created, but it is not recognized, defended, or scaled.

Part I breaks that gap open. It explains how effort became a proxy for value, why activity metrics persist even when they mislead, and how well-intentioned measurement often turns into theater. It explores why smart teams still lose funding, why dashboards fail to drive action, and why delivery success so often fails to influence prioritization.

Most importantly, it introduces a shift in mindset: from reporting work to quantifying contribution. From describing what was done to explaining what changed—and what that change is worth in time, money, risk, and opportunity.[2]

Before we introduce a framework, we need a shared diagnosis.

Because you can't fix invisible work until you understand why it disappeared in the first place.

CHAPTER 1

THE IMPACT GAP

"When I measure what I value, I make better decisions than when I value what I can measure."

— PETER DRUCKER

Why effort is mistaken for value

Most organizations don't intentionally reward the wrong things. They follow signals. And for decades, the loudest signal has been effort. Being busy. Being present. Being seen. Long hours, full calendars, late-night emails—these become shorthand for importance. Somewhere along the way, motion was confused with progress.

We've all seen it: the person pedaling furiously on a stationary bike, exhausted but unmoved. Or the colleague parked in their chair all day, clicking through spreadsheets, "working" without producing anything meaningful. Historically, organizations learned to equate presence with contribution because presence was easy to observe. Value was not.[1]

The problem is that this assumption collapses the moment decisions matter. If effort equals value, then more hours should mean more impact. Yet every major operating model—from Lean to Six Sigma—exists for one reason: to remove waste. If effort alone created value, process optimization would be unnecessary. The very existence of efficiency frameworks proves the opposite.

When leaders are forced to choose—what to fund, what to cut, what to prioritize—they don't trust effort. They trust evidence. And there is one form of evidence that transcends role, function, and opinion: dollars.[2]

You can describe a weekend of hard work in vivid detail, but it won't land. Say instead, "I saved $225 by not hiring pest control and lawn services," and suddenly everyone understands. Whether it took one hour or sixteen no longer matters. The outcome does.

This is the first hard truth of quantifying value: Effort may accompany value, but it does not define it. Until work is translated into economic impact, it remains noise—well-intentioned, exhausting, and ultimately disposable.

How work becomes invisible at scale

As organizations grow, something strange happens: Hero work disappears. The very tasks that once made someone indispensable—chasing issues, stitching systems together, manually fixing breakdowns—slowly fade from view. Not because they weren't valuable, but because scale absorbs them.

Consolidation, automation, new platforms, and standardized processes eliminate entire categories of effort. What once required vigilance now happens quietly in the background. The institutional wizard who knew every workaround suddenly looks...idle. Three years ago, they were a top performer. Today, leaders are asking, "What do they even do?"

Specialization accelerates this invisibility. In smaller organizations, everyone wears 10 hats. In larger ones, you may wear one—and only the people standing directly in front of you can see it. Functional blinders form. If your work doesn't intersect someone's immediate accountability, it may as well not exist.[3]

This is where the danger sharpens. Invisible work doesn't get debated during budget reviews—it gets cut. When times get tough, leaders don't eliminate what they don't value; they eliminate what they can't see. And visibility is not about effort—it's about articulation.

We've all lived the aftermath. Weeks after someone leaves, the realization hits: They owned everything. But by then, it's too late. The value walked out the door unrecorded, unmeasured, unprotected.

The lesson is uncomfortable but critical: You cannot rely on the organization to notice value. You have a responsibility to surface it. To translate invisible effort into visible impact. To package your contribution in a way that is clear, credible, and shareable—before scrutiny arrives.

The mismatch between delivery and decision-making

There's a quiet lie embedded in how most work gets done: If you plan well, execute cleanly, and deliver exactly to requirements, decisions will reward you accordingly. That's not how organizations actually operate.

Work is reported linearly—roadmaps, milestones, deliverables, status decks. Decisions, however, are anything but linear. They emerge through conversations, partial information, shifting context, and informal influence. By the time a document is polished, the decision may already be half-made.

Delivery success often fails to influence prioritization because it's evaluated through a different lens. Leaders don't ask, "Was this delivered?" They ask, "Does this matter now?" And that answer is shaped less by artifacts and more by trust networks.

Influence changes everything. If a business partner trusts you, your delivery range is wide—you can underdeliver or overdeliver and still be perceived as valuable. Without that trust, even flawless execution can be dismissed: technically correct, but no one's using it. Requirements met, but the business moved on.

What's missing at decision time isn't more detail—it's context. Specifically, the ability to explain why the work mattered economically when it mattered. That explanation must be simple enough to survive hallway conversations and strong enough to stand up to scrutiny.

This is where value articulation becomes decisive. If neither you nor your manager can translate delivery into impact in real time, the work loses its voice in the room where priorities are set.

Where value leaks in modern operating models

Most value isn't destroyed in dramatic failures. It leaks—quietly, repeatedly, and unmeasured—through the cracks of modern workflows.

Handoffs are the first fracture point. Every transition between teams introduces delay, interpretation risk, and rework. No one owns the whole outcome, only their slice. The cost accumulates invisibly, spread thin enough that no single group feels accountable.

Rework compounds the loss. Requirements change. Context shifts. Outputs technically meet specifications but miss the need. Each iteration consumes time, attention, and credibility—yet rarely gets quantified. The organization absorbs the cost as "just how things work."[4]

Why aren't these leaks measured? Because they live between org charts. They don't belong cleanly to a function, so they don't appear cleanly in reports. And because effort is visible while erosion is not, the system keeps rewarding activity instead of outcomes.

The irony is that leaders are desperate to stop this bleeding—but they need numbers to act. Without quantified deltas—time saved, dollars avoided, throughput increased—value erosion remains anecdotal. And anecdotes don't survive prioritization.

Until leaks are translated into economic terms, they are treated as inconvenience rather than opportunity. The work continues. The waste persists. And the organization unknowingly funds inefficiency year after year.

Why smart teams still lose funding

Everyone has seen it: a capable, high-performing team that somehow ends up defunded. It's rarely because the team failed. More often, it's because their value was never made explicit.

Smart teams assume leaders already know. They believe performance speaks for itself. But leaders oversee too much, too fast, with too little context. When budget decisions arrive, they don't recall effort—they recall narratives.

Value articulation overrides good performance every time. Just like resumes: one person carries deep expertise but summarizes it in bland bullet points. Another worked on a few visible projects and tells a compelling impact story. Guess who advances?

The pattern is consistent. Defunded teams deliver well, collaborate well, and remain busy—but cannot clearly answer one question: What would the organization lose if you disappeared tomorrow?

If that answer isn't quantified, it isn't defensible.

Reframing work as economic contribution

Everything changes when work is framed economically. Say "We improved a process," and interpretation varies. Say "We avoided $500,000 in annual cost," and everyone understands. They may debate the math—but not the meaning.

Economic framing aligns conversations instantly. It reshapes prioritization from opinion to trade-off. It allows leaders to compare unlike work on a common scale. And it gives your contribution a seat at the table where real decisions are made.

Resistance often shows up in three places: Inconsistency. Misalignment with organizational language. And failure to individualize impact. Overcome those, and value becomes durable—not dependent on visibility, politics, or memory.

This is the shift: from doing work to owning contribution. From effort to evidence. From activity to impact.

And once you can quantify your value, your work stops disappearing.

CHAPTER 2

FROM ACTIVITY TO OUTCOMES

"Never confuse motion with action."

— ERNEST HEMINGWAY

Activity metrics and why they persist

Activity metrics are everywhere because they are easy. Meetings held. Tickets closed. Reports generated. Emails sent. They measure observable motion—things you can count without waiting, debating causality, or arguing about impact. And that ease is precisely why they persist.

Activity metrics are politically safe. They are objective, auditable, and defensible in performance reviews. No one argues whether 10 meetings occurred. No one disputes that a report was delivered. For leaders, they provide a comforting illusion of control: Something is being measured, therefore something is being managed.[1]

The trouble begins once activity metrics get embedded into dashboards, compensation structures, and performance systems. Behavior starts to orbit the metric. People optimize for what is counted, not for what matters. At that point, removing the metric feels dangerous—like removing accountability itself. Few remember why the metric was created in the first place, but everyone knows their evaluation depends on it.[2]

There's also a quiet fear that if activity metrics disappear, nothing will replace them. The contrarian voice asks, "What else would we measure?" And so flawed metrics survive by default—not because they're good, but because they're familiar.

Organizations are incentivized to keep them because measuring impact is harder. Impact takes time. It requires waiting for outcomes, forming hypotheses, and admitting uncertainty. Counting activity avoids all of that. It's a race to safety: Measuring something feels better than measuring nothing, even when the signal is misleading.

That said, activity metrics are not useless. They can function as leading indicators when diagnosing how work gets done—not judging performance but understanding flow. They can matter for compliance, audit trails, and minimum engagement thresholds. Used this way, they are guardrails.

The problem is mistaking guardrails for goals. When activity becomes the destination, value quietly exits the system.

Outputs vs. outcomes vs. impact

Three concepts are constantly confused—and the confusion is costly: outputs, outcomes, and impact.

Outputs are what you produce. A dashboard. A model. A report. A release. They are tangible, deliverable, and easy to declare "done." Outcomes are different. Outcomes are the change that happens because the output exists—behavior shifts, decisions improve, costs decrease, revenue accelerates.[3]

Impact goes one step further. Impact translates those outcomes into economic or strategic consequence. It answers the question leaders actually care about: So what did this change mean for the organization?

Most teams stop at outputs. Take a familiar example. A data team builds a polished Power BI dashboard for Sales—15 visuals, daily refresh, clean Snowflake integration. Stakeholders love the demo. The project is marked successful and closed.

Six weeks later, usage logs tell a different story. Three of 40 intended users have logged in. One uses it regularly. Everyone else still exports data to Excel and complains about visibility. The output exists. The outcome did not.

Where teams most often fall short is assuming delivery equals value. Once the artifact is shipped, accountability dissolves. Adoption, behavior change, and downstream results become someone else's problem.

When impact becomes the goal, the work changes. Teams stay engaged past delivery. Success is measured later, not sooner. Questions shift from "Did we build it?" to "Did it change anything?" and eventually to "Was the change worth it?"[4]

This shift is uncomfortable because it removes the safety of completion. You can't hide behind artifacts. But it's also where work becomes defensible, fundable, and strategically relevant.[5]

Why dashboards fail to change decisions

Dashboards fail for one primary reason: they assume visibility creates action. If people can see the data, they will respond to it. This assumption is almost always false.

Most dashboards also assume users know which questions to ask, how to interpret trends, and whether up is good or down is bad. They assume people have time to explore. They assume insight naturally creates urgency.

In reality, people see problems constantly, and do nothing. Awareness is not the constraint—friction is.

Dashboards rarely show the cost of action. They don't reveal the political capital required, the difficult conversations ahead, or the reputational risk of admitting prior decisions were wrong. A dashboard might clearly expose a forecasting error, but fixing it may require confronting three managers, reallocating resources, and explaining to leadership why last quarter's numbers were incorrect.[6]

The dashboard surfaces the issue. It does nothing to reduce the resistance to responding.

Another failure is context. Dashboards are directional, not definitive. They show trends without translating magnitude. Leaders are left asking: Is this worth acting on right now? Without economic framing, the answer is often no.[7]

This is why more visibility rarely equals more action. Dashboards inform. Decisions demand justification.

Until insights are paired with quantified consequences—dollars at risk, capacity constrained, opportunity cost incurred—the dashboard remains passive. Useful, but inert. Data doesn't drive decisions. Trade-offs do.[8]

OKRs, KPIs, and measurement theater

Assigning a metric does not mean something is under control. Often, it means the opposite. Metrics can create the illusion of management without the reality of influence.[9]

Precision feels like accuracy. A dashboard shows 70% customer satisfaction, and everyone relaxes—until you realize only 5% of customers responded. The number is precise, but the signal is weak. Yet the visual certainty creates psychological comfort.

Another illusion is causation. When a metric improves, teams assume their actions caused it. Sometimes the number would have moved anyway. Correlation masquerades as control, and learning stops prematurely.

Then there's the flight to green. Status indicators drift toward "on track" even as systems quietly degrade in unmeasured ways. From an OKR or KPI perspective, everything looks healthy—until it isn't.

OKRs fail when they stop being stretch goals. Instead of aiming for breakthrough, teams sandbag. If 70% attainment is considered success, delivery is calibrated to hit 65–70%, not 90. Real innovation gets traded for predictable optics.

Measurement theater emerges when organizations measure what's convenient instead of what's meaningful. The hardest metrics—those tied to customer pain, adoption, or economic value—often require stitching data across systems and making assumptions. That work is avoided. Easier proxies take their place.

The result is a dashboard full of activity and compliance, with very little truth about value. Everything is measured. Very little is understood.

Shifting from reporting to quantification

Reporting and quantification are not the same, though they're often treated as interchangeable.

Reporting tells you what happened: "Region 3 sales are down 12%." It's backward-looking, technically accurate, and assumption-free. Quantification tells you what it means: "That decline represents a $2.4M revenue gap and an 18% reduction in bonus potential if unaddressed."

Reporting shows the dashboard. Quantification connects the dashboard to a decision.

This shift requires assumptions—and that's why it's avoided. Quantification is forward-looking. It estimates scenarios, infers consequences, and asks, "How much?" and "So what?" It trades certainty for usefulness.

Data alone can't answer decision questions. Should we invest in improving onboarding? Data can show completion rates and churn. The decision requires assumptions: If onboarding improves, how much will completion rise? If completion rises, how much churn will drop? Those links must be modeled, not observed.

Quantified insights are more actionable because they translate observations into the language decisions are made in: money, time, risk, and trade-offs. They clarify thresholds for action.

Instead of asking, "Is the trend good or bad?" leaders ask, "Is this worth fixing now?" That's the difference.

Yes, quantification means being wrong—but in traceable ways. Assumptions are documented. Models can be refined. Learning compounds.

Reporting describes the past. Quantification makes the future discussable.

What it means to "own" an outcome

Owning an outcome is fundamentally different from delivering an output. Outputs end at completion. Outcomes extend into reality.

When you own an outcome, you are accountable for whether the work actually changes something. In the earlier dashboard example, delivery was perfect—but adoption failed. That is not a successful outcome.

True ownership involves staying engaged past delivery, accepting ambiguous accountability, measuring what matters rather than what flatters, and adapting when conditions change. It means you don't stop when the box is checked—you stop when the result materializes.

This level of ownership reshapes behavior. Teams prioritize differently. Low-value work gets cut. Quality standards rise because downstream consequences are visible. Cross-functional friction becomes your problem to solve, not someone else's excuse.

Language changes too. Conversations move from, "We completed X" to, "Here's what we're seeing, what it means, and what we're trying next." Teams begin to sound like owners, not operators.

So why is ownership avoided? Because it's risky. Outcomes aren't fully controllable. Failure becomes personal. There's nowhere to hide when results don't land.

Timing also works against ownership. Outcomes often materialize outside performance cycles. Adoption might spike after reviews are closed. On paper, the work looks unsuccessful—even if reality says otherwise.

Ownership is high-status in theory and high-stakes in practice. But it's also the only place where work becomes durable, defensible, and worth funding.

And that is the trade: safety versus significance.

CHAPTER 3

THE LANGUAGE OF BUSINESS VALUE

"Try not to become a person of success, but rather try to become a person of value."

— ALBERT EINSTEIN

Time as a measurable asset

When people talk about "business value," they reach for the usual vocabulary: cashable benefits, non-cashable benefits, headcount reduction, revenue lift. What rarely gets named—despite being the thing every leader is desperate to find more of—is time.[1]

Time is undervalued because it doesn't show up on the balance sheet. You can't "spend" time from a budget line the way you spend dollars. You can't deplete it in a system of record. And because organizations reward the appearance of busyness, time waste often looks like importance. A packed calendar becomes a humble brag: I must be critical. Meanwhile, speed isn't directly measured. Most places track what got produced, not how long it took—or how long it should have taken.[2]

That's how you end up with a simple data product taking nine and a half months and four people and nobody blinking because "it shipped." The output is visible. The time cost is not.

The fix isn't complicated—but it requires consistency. Time can be measured through cycle time tracking, time allocation analysis, process mapping, or fully loaded cost models. You can track average turnaround time, time-to-value, queue time, rework time, and handoff delays. The method matters less than applying the same method repeatedly, so trends become undeniable.[3]

Of course, not all time saved matters. Saving 10 hours this week doesn't magically turn into innovation unless the savings are big enough to change behavior. But when reclaimed time crosses a threshold—when it removes chronic bottlenecks, reduces overtime, prevents backlog growth, or frees capacity for higher-value work—time becomes the most practical asset you can deliver.[4]

That's the reframing: Time isn't "soft." Time is capacity. And capacity is strategy.

Cost, avoidance, and opportunity cost

To quantify value credibly, you need to separate three terms that people constantly blur: direct cost, cost avoidance, and opportunity cost. They sound similar. They are not.[5]

Direct cost is simple: Money leaves the account. There's an invoice, a wire transfer, a GL line item. Spend $100,000 on a software license, and finance trusts it because it's observable, repeatable, and undeniable.

Cost avoidance is different. It's money you would have spent but didn't because of an intervention. It's counterfactual by nature—claiming credit for a future expense that never appears. Renegotiate a contract and avoid an 8% annual uplift? That's real value, but you won't see a line on the GL that says, "Congrats, you didn't spend this." That invisibility is why cost avoidance lives in the gray zone between real savings and wishful thinking.[6]

Opportunity cost is the most strategic of the three. It isn't about what you spent or avoided. It's the value you gave up by choosing one path over the best alternative. If your team spent four months automating a process, the opportunity cost is whatever else they could have built in those four months—especially if the alternative would have produced greater value.

Here's the clearest way to see all three at once: A manual process costs $200,000/year in labor (direct cost). Automation costs $80,000 to build (direct cost). If it works, you avoid $200,000/year of ongoing labor (cost avoidance). But if those same engineers could have built a revenue feature worth an estimated $500,000, that's the opportunity cost of choosing automation over growth.[7]

Cost avoidance is often misunderstood because it's easy to inflate: Baselines get manipulated, "savings" don't free cash, and incentives push people to overclaim. That's why assumptions must be documented. Opportunity cost strengthens value claims because it forces honesty: not just "Is this good?" but "Is this the best use of our time?"

Risk, volatility, and downside protection

Leaders don't fear bad outcomes in the abstract. They fear the kind of bad outcome they can't explain.

Unmanaged risk creates two problems: the event itself and the story that follows it. When something goes wrong—an outage, a data breach, a compliance failure—the pain isn't only operational. It's reputational. It's the executive standing in front of a board or regulator trying to justify why the organization didn't see it coming. Volatility is what keeps leaders awake: not predictable costs, but unpredictable failures.[8]

Risk becomes quantifiable the moment you can estimate two things: probability and severity. How likely is it to happen, and how bad would it be if it did? If you can estimate frequency—once a month, once a quarter, once a year—and pair it with a severity model—direct financial cost, revenue impact, operational disruption, reputational damage—you can produce an expected loss estimate. It won't be perfect. It will be useful.

This is where explaining assumptions matters more than pretending certainty. Leaders don't require perfect probabilities; they require coherent logic. If you say, "This failure pattern happens about four times a year, and each incident costs us roughly $150,000 in labor, downtime, and customer remediation," you've given them something they can reason with—even if the range is wide.

There are moments when risk reduction outweighs savings, and it's not subtle. A $200,000 efficiency improvement can be dwarfed by a $2M downside event with even modest probability. And in regulated environments, the severity may include non-financial consequences—loss of license, legal exposure, forced audits—that make the risk intolerable even when the expected value math seems "fine."[9]

Quantifying risk is not about fearmongering. It's about making the invisible visible: translating volatility into decision language. Because once leaders can see downside clearly, "nice-to-have" work suddenly becomes protection—and protection gets funded.

Scale, frequency, and compounding effects

Most people overvalue big wins and undervalue repeated wins. That's backwards. In real systems, frequency often matters more than size.

Consider two improvements: Process A saves 30 minutes on a task performed twice a year. That's one hour annually. Process B saves two minutes on a task performed 500 times a year. That's 1,000 minutes—16.7 hours annually. Process A sounds more impressive. Process B is almost invisible. Yet Process B delivers over 16 times the value.

This pattern is everywhere: Small frictions at scale become major cost. A tiny error rate multiplied across thousands of transactions becomes a serious exposure. A minor delay in onboarding multiplied across cohorts becomes churn. A slightly confusing customer flow multiplied across millions of users becomes a product problem. High-frequency decisions compound quietly—and because the pain is distributed, no one feels the full weight until it's huge.

Scale amplifies everything. A one-person time save is nice. A team-wide time save is capacity. A department-wide improvement is strategy. Whether you scale by people (headcount), transactions, customers, tickets, or revenue events, the math changes dramatically once you stop thinking in single instances and start thinking in systems.[10]

The compounding effects most often ignored are second-order. People see the immediate time saved but miss what it unlocks: faster cycles reduce backlog growth; fewer handoffs reduce rework; fewer defects reduce customer escalations; less volatility reduces management overhead; higher adoption increases ROI on everything downstream. Improvements don't just add—they cascade.

Linear thinking is intuitive. Exponential thinking is not. That's why frequency and scale are the quantifier's advantage: They turn "small" into "inevitable." When you can show how a two-minute reduction multiplies into weeks of reclaimed capacity across a year, value stops being a story. It becomes arithmetic.

And arithmetic is hard to argue with.

Precision over perfection in value claims

If you're a perfectionist, value quantification will challenge you—because perfect accuracy is not available.

Most value models are future-facing. They rely on incomplete information about the present and uncertain assumptions about human behavior, market movement, and system response. Causation is murky. Inputs are noisy. Even measurement instruments—surveys, logs, time tracking, attribution—are imperfect. The idea that you can produce a single exact number, down to the dollar, is not just unrealistic. It's conceptually misleading.

The goal is not perfection. The goal is decision-grade precision.

Your precision should match your certainty. If this is the first time you've run a process, don't present value to the penny as if you're reading it from a ledger. Instead of "$4,847,285 saved," say "roughly $4–5M" or "about $4.8M, with a reasonable range." That signals two things at once: You did the math, and you're not pretending to know what can't be known.

Ranges build trust because they reflect reality. Executives live in ranges: best case, worst case, most likely. When you give a pessimistic, likely, and optimistic scenario, you're showing you understand conditions can change—adoption might lag, usage might spike, or constraints might emerge. It doesn't weaken your claim. It strengthens it.

A practical approach is to show an executive roll-up—clean, simple, high-level—and keep the detailed math in an appendix. Almost no one reads it, but when someone wants to pressure test your logic, you have receipts. Assumptions are documented. Inputs are visible. The model is traceable.

Being wrong is acceptable. Being vague is not. Precision over perfection means you're willing to estimate, own your assumptions, and refine later. That's how quantification becomes credible—and usable.

Translating work into executive language

Executives operate under limited attention, relentless demand, and accountability for outcomes they don't fully control. That reality shapes what gets heard.

There are two universal triggers for executive attention: money and time. Mention either, and you get engagement. Mention both—tied to an outcome—and you get action.

This is why executive language consistently prioritizes outcomes over activities. "We migrated to a new platform" is an activity. Most leaders won't care—because it doesn't tell them what changed. "We reduced processing time by 40%, which unblocked $2M in delayed revenue" is an outcome. Now you're speaking the language of trade-offs and consequence.[11]

Technical work must be reframed the same way. A new data pipeline isn't the point. The point is reduced manual labor, faster decision cycles, improved forecast accuracy, fewer defects, lower incident risk, higher conversion, lower churn. Technical achievement is the mechanism. Executives fund the result.[12]

The language that immediately weakens credibility is effort language and insider language: "We worked really hard." "We delivered a robust solution." "We completed a migration." "We held stakeholder sessions." Those may be true, but they force the executive to translate them into impact—and they won't. Not because they don't care, but because they don't have time.

Strong executive framing is simple: what changed, how much it changed, and what that change is worth. Use money, time, risk, and trade-offs. Be clear about assumptions. Give ranges. Anchor to decisions.

When you translate your work this way, you stop competing for attention. You start competing for priority.

PART II

THE QUANTIFIED IMPACT FRAMEWORK™

Part II is where this book becomes operational.

Up to this point, we've talked about why value is hard to articulate, why good work often goes unrecognized, and why most organizations default to vague language when they should be speaking in measurable terms. But insight alone doesn't change conversations. A repeatable method does.

That's what the Quantified Impact Framework™ is.

This is not a finance-heavy model built for capital allocation decisions. It's not a business case template. It's a practitioner framework—built for the "everything else" work that keeps organizations moving: process improvements, analytics, automation, enablement, and system changes that rarely get formal ROI treatment but still create real impact.

The framework is intentionally simple: define the "before" state, define the "after" state, measure what changed, and scale that change into business language. It forces discipline without forcing complexity. It's designed to be used in real time with real teams using real assumptions that can be explained and defended.

In the chapters that follow, we'll walk step-by-step through the framework—starting with how to establish a credible baseline, then how to describe the new reality, then how to calculate deltas without overstating them. From there, we'll annualize and scale value responsibly, and finally, we'll make sure every claim can survive scrutiny.

Because the goal isn't just quantified impact.

It's trusted impact.

CHAPTER 4

INTRODUCING THE QUANTIFIED IMPACT FRAMEWORK™

"All models are wrong, but some are useful."

— GEORGE E. P. COX

Why one framework beats many methods

If you've been around value conversations long enough, you've seen the alphabet soup: Net present value, internal rate of return, modified IRR, payback period, discounted cash flow, cost–benefit analysis, cashable versus non-cashable benefits. None of these are wrong. In fact, they are extremely powerful tools when applied in the right context, for the right decisions, and at the right level of scale.[1]

The problem is not the math. The problem is overfitting complexity to work that simply doesn't require it.

Most initiatives we touch in our day-to-day work are not five-year, $500-million transformation programs. They are process changes. Reporting improvements. Automation. Better access to data. Workflow redesign. Enablement initiatives that improve how work gets done rather than what the company owns.

Yet we routinely try to force this type of work into investment-grade financial models designed for capital allocation decisions.

That's where confusion begins.

Different stakeholders gravitate toward different lenses. Finance often wants rigor and defensibility. Leaders want clarity and speed. Practitioners want something practical that doesn't take weeks to assemble. The result is a patchwork of methods, each applied inconsistently depending on who is in the room.[2]

And when there are many frameworks, there is effectively no framework at all.

What I'm proposing here is not a replacement for enterprise investment governance. This is not how you decide whether to acquire a company, build a plant, or launch a multi-year transformation program. Those decisions deserve formal business cases and sophisticated financial modeling.

This framework exists for everything else.

It is designed for individuals, teams, and practitioners who need a consistent way to quantify the value of the work they already do—work that often falls below the threshold of formal investment analysis but still matters deeply to the organization.

One framework beats many methods because it creates a shared language. It removes unnecessary interpretation. It lowers the barrier to entry without lowering credibility. People don't need to debate discount rates or reinvestment assumptions to understand impact.

Instead, we focus on what actually changed.

Before, something took time, effort, or cost.

After, it took less.

That difference matters.

The framework works precisely because it is narrow by design. It fits the majority of initiatives that sit below formal business cases but still deserve to be measured. When people can apply the same logic repeatedly, across initiatives and over time, trust builds. Comparability improves. Confidence grows.

One framework doesn't oversimplify value.

It operationalizes it.

Before we go further, here is the core framework you'll see referenced throughout the rest of this chapter (and the chapters that follow). It's intentionally simple and repeatable: start by describing reality, then measure what changed, then scale it into business impact. If you remember nothing else, remember this sequence—it's the backbone of every defensible value claim in this book.

Quantify Value Framework

1. Define "before" state
2. Define "after" state
3. Map process steps
4. Identify actors
5. Capture frequency
6. Capture effort per step
7. Scale across time (week → month → year)
8. Apply blended rate
9. Calculate deltas
10. Translate into business language

You don't need a different method for every situation. You need one shared logic that works across most real-world initiatives—especially the "everything else" work that rarely gets a formal business case but still creates meaningful impact.

The Quantified Impact Framework™

A SYSTEMATIC METHODOLOGY FOR TRANSLATING INITIATIVES INTO MEASURABLE BUSINESS VALUE

1 **Define Before State**
Establish the measurable baseline before your initiative. What was the count, cost, risk level, or time expenditure?

2 **Define After State**
Document the measurable outcome after your initiative. Use the same metrics as your Before State for direct comparison.

3 **Map Process Steps**
Identify each discrete activity—both old and new processes. This reveals where time and effort are consumed.

4 **Identify Actors**
Who performs each step? This determines cost basis and reveals cross-functional dependencies and collaboration opportunities.

5 **Capture Frequency**
How often does each step occur? This is the multiplier that scales individual effort into organizational impact.

6 **Capture Effort per Step**
Quantify time for each step. Be specific: "approximately 2 hours" beats "some time." Include setup and follow-up.

7 **Scale Across Time**
Extend calculations to annual impact: Week □ Month □ Year. Executives think in annual budgets; speak their language.

8 **Apply Blended Rate**
Convert hours to dollars using blended labor rate. Include salary, benefits, and overhead. $75–150/hr is typical for IT.

9 **Calculate Deltas**
Compute the difference between Before and After states. This is your quantified impact: cost avoided, hours saved.

10 **Translate into Business Language**
Convert technical metrics into executive-ready language. "Reduced attack surface" □ "eliminated 12 breach entry points."

COST AVOIDANCE · RISK REDUCTION · OPERATIONAL EFFICIENCY

Figure 4.1 The Quantified Impact Framework™

The Before → After → Delta → Scale logic

Every credible measurement starts with a baseline. Yet in practice, baseline thinking is often the first thing abandoned when discussing value. We jump straight to solutions, benefits, and outcomes without anchoring the conversation in what actually existed before the change.

This framework deliberately forces discipline by starting with the before state.

Before is not a vague recollection or a high-level summary. It is a concrete description of reality. What steps occurred? Who performed them? How many steps were there—eight, 10, sometimes more? Even when people say there was "no process," informal workarounds almost always existed.[3]

Someone, somewhere, was doing something.

Documenting the before state makes invisible effort visible. It also prevents inflated claims later by grounding the analysis in facts rather than memory, perception, or hindsight bias.

Once the before state is clear, we pivot to the after state. The same lens. The same level of detail. This is critical. The goal is not to describe aspirations or design intent but actual execution. What steps exist now? Who performs them? How does the work really happen today?[4]

The form of the change doesn't matter. It could be a new system, a Power BI report, an automation, a redesigned process, or a new operating model. What matters is that before and after are comparable.

Without both, you cannot measure change. This is no different than managing a project without a baseline schedule and wondering whether you're late. Without a baseline, deviation is unknowable.

Once both states are defined, delta becomes inevitable. Delta is simply the difference between two comparable realities. Fewer steps. Less effort. Shorter cycle time. Reduced rework. Improved throughput. These differences are not theoretical—they are observable.

This is where most value hides, often in plain sight.

If 10 steps become eight, that's not a story. That's a measurable efficiency change.

Finally, we scale. How often does this process occur? How many people are involved? How many teams, regions, or business units are affected? This is where individual improvements compound into enterprise-level impact.

Before. After. Delta. Scale.

It's simple, not simplistic—and because it compares apples to apples, it stands up under scrutiny.

What the framework intentionally ignores

One of the most important design choices in this framework is what it intentionally does not try to measure. This is where many value models lose credibility, not because they are wrong but because they overreach.

Most notably, the framework avoids claiming "cost saved."

That phrase triggers scrutiny for good reason. If a process takes 10 hours today and now takes five, we did not magically remove headcount from the balance sheet. No one was fired. No budget line disappeared. The organization did not suddenly spend less cash.[5]

What we created instead is cost avoided and capacity released.

Those five hours can now be redeployed to higher-value work, absorbed growth, or reduce future hiring pressure. That outcome is real, but it is different from cost savings. This distinction matters because it keeps the conversation honest and defensible.

We are not promising financial outcomes that require organizational actions outside our control. We are quantifying change that actually occurred.

The framework also intentionally ignores many traditional investment metrics—not because they lack value but because they introduce friction where it isn't needed. Discount rates, capital structures, multi-year cash flow projections, and reinvestment assumptions belong in board-level investment decisions, not day-to-day impact tracking.

When practitioners are forced into those models, value becomes fragile. Easy to challenge. Easy to dismiss. Easy to derail.

By contrast, time reduced from 10 hours to five is difficult to argue with. Cycle time reduced from 30 days to 20 is observable. Effort eliminated is tangible.[6]

The framework also avoids speculative benefits. There is no "potential revenue," no assumed adoption curves, and no hockey-stick projections. If it happened, we measure it. If it didn't, we don't.

That constraint is not a limitation. It is a feature.

It keeps the framework repeatable, defensible, and trusted—especially by finance partners who are tired of theoretical numbers that never materialize.

Ignoring complexity here is not laziness.

It is focus.

How this differs from ROI and business cases

Business cases serve an important and necessary purpose. They help organizations decide whether to invest. They consider total cost of ownership, capital versus operating expense, fixed versus variable costs, and cashability. For those decisions, formal ROI measures like NPV, IRR, and payback are extremely useful.[7]

But they answer a different question.

ROI and business cases are designed to evaluate potential value before something exists.

This framework is designed to measure realized value after change has occurred.

Instead of constructing a broad financial narrative, we focus on a narrow operational reality. A process. A system.

A workflow. A capability. We ask a simple but powerful question: What changed because we did this?

In many cases, the financial investment behind these initiatives is negligible, already embedded in existing budgets, or simply not worth modeling in detail. Forcing a full ROI analysis in those situations slows momentum and dilutes credibility.

This framework deliberately operates over realistic time horizons—weeks, months, or quarters—not multi-year projections. That makes it especially effective for analytics, automation, IT enablement, and continuous improvement work.

You're not asking for permission to invest.

You're proving that value was delivered.

That distinction fundamentally changes the conversation. ROI argues for funding. This framework demonstrates contribution. Both matter, but they belong at different moments in the lifecycle of work.

When to apply the framework

This framework works anytime you can clearly define a before state and an after state. That is the only real requirement, yet it is often overlooked.

Most conversations do not start there. Leaders jump to solutions. Teams jump to features. Everyone wants to talk about what's new, improved, or delivered. The risk is that we skip the very context that makes value measurable.[8]

Resist that instinct.

Always pull the conversation back to the basics: What actually happened before this existed? What steps occurred? Who did the work? How often did it happen? How long did it take?

Only once that picture is clear should you discuss the change.

Applying the framework early prevents solution bias. Applying it after implementation ensures credibility. In both cases, it creates alignment.

This approach is especially valuable when initiatives feel "obviously valuable" but are hard to articulate. Those are precisely the situations where value gets assumed instead of measured.

Yes, parts of this work feel boring. Process mapping is not glamorous. Counting steps isn't exciting. But this discipline is what turns opinions into evidence.[9]

If you've ever joined a meeting halfway through and struggled to understand what's going on you understand the risk of skipping the beginning. Start with the full picture.

Before. After. Delta.

Everything else follows.

How the framework builds trust

Trust is built when people understand and believe the numbers. This framework earns trust because it is intuitive, transparent, and repeatable.

At its simplest, the logic requires no translation. A process took 25 hours. Now it takes 10. Most people understand that immediately, without financial interpretation or technical explanation.

The framework also separates effort from duration. A task may require 10 hours of work but span 30 days end-to-end due to handoffs, dependencies, or waiting time. Reducing either dimension creates value, and the framework captures both explicitly.[10]

Because the logic is consistent, results become comparable across initiatives. Stakeholders don't have to relearn a new model each time. Finance doesn't have to reinterpret assumptions. Leaders don't have to decode jargon.

This consistency reduces friction and accelerates acceptance.

The framework also invites participation. Before and after states are defined collaboratively with the people doing the work, not imposed from outside. That inclusion improves accuracy and builds ownership.[11]

When people see their reality reflected accurately, they accept the outcome faster.

Over time, this repeatability compounds. Value conversations become easier, faster, and less defensive. The organization stops debating whether value exists and starts discussing how to scale it.

That is the real payoff.

Not just quantified impact—but trusted impact.

CHAPTER 5

DEFINING THE BEFORE STATE

"The reward of a thing well done is to have done it."

— RALPH WALDO EMERSON

Identifying the real process boundary

When defining the before state, the first and most important question is deceptively simple: Where does this process actually start, and where does it end? That sounds straightforward, but in practice, it's where many value discussions go off track.

If you step back and think about the continuity of running a business, processes never really stop. From the first day a company exists to the day it is sold, merged, or shut down, work flows continuously. There are thousands—sometimes hundreds of thousands—of interconnected processes operating at any given time.[1]

What we are not trying to do is map all of that.

The goal here is to identify the specific process boundary that matters for the change you are measuring. That boundary is usually much smaller than people initially assume. It may be three steps. It may be 10. Rarely does it need to be more.

When you ask a stakeholder, "What did you do before this system or process existed?" the answer is often informal. "We didn't really have anything. Mary and Mohammed worked together and figured it out." That response is not wrong—but it's incomplete.[2]

Your job is to unpack it.

What exactly did Mary do? What did Mohammed do next? What triggered the work to start, and what signaled that it was finished? Those are the real boundaries of the process.

At the same time, you need restraint. Every process touches upstream and downstream activities. Including every fringe interaction quickly turns a simple baseline into an unusable map. You are not documenting the enterprise. You are defining the slice that changed.

A good process boundary captures the work that would no longer need to happen—or would happen differently—after the change. If it doesn't change, it probably doesn't belong in the boundary.

Clear boundaries are what make the rest of the framework possible. Without them, effort bleeds in from everywhere, and the before state loses credibility.

Mapping steps, handoffs, and rework

Once the process boundary is defined, the next step is to map what actually happens inside it. This is where many practitioners default to "happy path" thinking—and where most value gets understated.[3]

Process steps are not just technical actions like generating a dataset, transforming data, or analyzing results. They include coordination, communication, waiting, and validation. All of that takes effort and time.

In many real-world processes, work does not flow linearly. Teams operate cross-functionally. One group cannot proceed until another provides input. That other group, in turn, may be waiting on something else. These predecessors and successors extend cycle time and create critical-path delays, regardless of how efficient any single step might be.

Those handoffs matter.

If you are working in a Six Sigma or Lean environment, this is simply another way of describing process duration and waste. If you are not, the principle still applies: Every dependency stretches the timeline.

Rework is another major component that is often overlooked. In reporting and analytics especially, data is rarely right the first time. Teams pull numbers from multiple sources, reconcile inconsistencies, receive feedback that "the numbers don't look right," and then adjust.[4]

That rework consumes hours—sometimes weekly, sometimes monthly.

When a new system creates a single source of truth, the value is not just faster report generation. It is the elimination of refactoring, correction, and validation cycles that were previously invisible.

All of that belongs in the before state.

If you don't capture rework, you are only measuring part of the problem—and undervaluing the solution.

Capturing effort by role and frequency

Effort alone is not enough. You also need to understand who is expending that effort and how often.

Different roles participate in the same process very differently. A sales representative may touch a process once per opportunity. An operations analyst may engage daily. A finance reviewer may only be involved monthly or quarterly.

That variation matters.

When capturing the before state, you should identify roles, not individuals. Sales, operations, finance, IT, marketing, supply chain—whatever is relevant. Then determine how frequently each role participates and how much effort they expend when they do.

For example, a sales team may spend 30 minutes per deal pulling data, while a finance team spends four hours per month reconciling totals. Both are part of the same process, but their effort profiles are entirely different.

Another common example is leadership involvement. A manager may only spend 15 minutes reviewing outputs, but if that review triggers rework, the downstream effort multiplies.

Frequency is what turns minutes into meaningful impact.

Without it, effort looks small and insignificant. With it, patterns emerge that explain where time and cost actually accumulate.

Capturing effort by role and frequency also sets up later scaling. When you expand from one team to 10, or one region to five, these distinctions become essential.

This is where baseline credibility begins to solidify.

Identifying friction and failure points

Let's be direct: If the before-state process worked flawlessly, there would be no reason to change it. Every improvement initiative exists because something, somewhere, is breaking down. Those breakdowns are not edge cases—they are part of how the current system actually operates.[5]

This is why identifying friction and failure points is not optional when defining the before state. It is essential.

Friction shows up in many forms. Sometimes it is obvious, like recurring errors, missed deadlines, or customer complaints. Other times it is quieter: manual reconciliations, shadow spreadsheets, follow-up emails, or recurring "just to be safe" checks layered onto the process over time.

These compensating behaviors are signals. They exist because the process cannot be trusted to run cleanly end to end.

Quarterly rework is a common example. A process may appear stable on a monthly basis, but every quarter, the team pauses normal work to reconcile data, validate assumptions, or explain discrepancies. That effort is often treated as "part of the job," yet it represents real time, real effort, and real cost.[6]

Exception handling is another frequent failure point. Processes are often designed for the average case, not the real one. When volumes spike, inputs change, or dependencies slip, people intervene manually to keep things moving. That intervention is not free.

The same is true for escalations. When leaders need to get involved to unblock work, review outputs, or resolve disputes, their time becomes part of the before-state cost—whether it was ever labeled that way or not.

Ignoring these failure points produces an artificially clean baseline. It understates effort and overstates process effectiveness. More importantly, it disconnects the quantified value from lived experience. When stakeholders read a baseline that excludes their pain points, credibility suffers immediately.

Capturing friction is not about assigning blame. It is about acknowledging reality. The before state must reflect not just how the process was designed to work but how it actually worked under real conditions.

When friction and failure are included, the baseline becomes honest. And honest baselines are the foundation of trusted impact.

Establishing credible baseline assumptions

No before-state model is free of assumptions. The question is not whether assumptions exist but whether they are explicit, reasonable, and validated. This is where many otherwise strong analyses lose trust.[7]

Assumptions often show up around people and scale. How many individuals were involved? Were they dedicated or part-time contributors? Did five people truly support the process, or did it touch 45 people for small increments of time?

Both scenarios can be true—and they have very different implications.

A common mistake is oversimplification. Collapsing complex participation into a single "team" may make the model cleaner, but it disconnects it from reality. Conversely, modeling every micro-interaction adds noise without clarity. The goal is a credible middle ground.[8]

Baseline assumptions should reflect how the business would describe itself. When stakeholders read your assumptions, they should recognize their own operating model immediately. If they pause or hesitate, that's a signal the assumptions need refinement.

Another critical area is change assumptions. If the before state involved three teams and the after state involves one, that shift must be clearly stated. If effort moves from senior roles to junior roles, that matters later when rates are applied.

Assumptions must also be time-bound. Was this process stable over the last year, or did volumes fluctuate? Were there seasonal spikes? Was the "average" month really average?

Documenting these nuances prevents challenges later.

Most importantly, assumptions should be validated with the business—not just shared but confirmed. This does not require formal sign-off, but it does require acknowledgment. A simple, "Yes, that reflects how we operated," is often enough.

Credible assumptions act as guardrails. They prevent overstatement. They protect against skepticism. And they ensure that when value is calculated later, the business sees it as a reflection of truth, not interpretation.

Documenting the before state defensibly

The final step in defining the before state is documentation—but not documentation for its own sake. The objective here is defensibility, not bureaucracy.

A defensible before state answers a simple question: Could someone else follow your logic and reach the same conclusion?

That requires clarity: What was included. What was excluded. Why certain steps mattered and others didn't. How effort, frequency, and roles were determined. Where friction and failure were accounted for.[9]

This does not mean creating a 100-slide deck or an overly detailed process map. In fact, overdocumentation often obscures insight rather than strengthening it. The goal is traceability, not volume.

A strong before-state document tells a coherent story. It connects process steps to effort. It ties roles to frequency. It explains assumptions without defensiveness. And it makes clear that the baseline reflects reality as it existed before any changes were made.[10]

This documentation also protects the work over time. People change roles. Context fades. Six months later, the rationale behind a number may be forgotten. A defensible baseline preserves that context, so value doesn't erode with memory.

It also enables comparison. When before states are documented consistently across initiatives, patterns emerge. Leaders begin to see where effort concentrates. Finance begins to trust the methodology. Practitioners begin to reuse and refine rather than reinvent.

Perhaps most importantly, defensible documentation shifts conversations. Instead of debating whether the baseline is valid, stakeholders focus on what changed and how to scale it.

That is the real power of doing this well.

A clear, credible before state is not just the starting point of the framework. It is the anchor that holds the entire value story in place.

CHAPTER 6

DESIGNING THE AFTER STATE

"The secret of change is to focus all of your energy not on fighting the old but on building the new."

— SOCRATES

What actually changes in the process?

When designing the after state, one of the most important mindset shifts is this: We no longer care about what used to happen. The before state has already done its job. At this point, the only thing that matters is what happens now.

That sounds obvious, but in practice, people constantly blur the two. They explain the after state by referencing how things used to work, which muddies the analysis and weakens the comparison. The after state must stand on its own.[1]

What you are trying to capture is the set of activities an individual performs today to execute the work, given that the system, process, or transformation is now fully in place. Not the rollout period. Not the transition phase. The steady state.

For example, consider an analyst. Before, they may have logged into five different systems, extracted data manually, reconciled inconsistencies, and built a report from scratch. In the after state, that analyst may log into a single dashboard, apply a filter, and review the output. That is the after state. Nothing else matters.

A business manager provides a different perspective. Before, they may have waited days for reports, followed up repeatedly, and questioned data accuracy. In the after state, they open a report themselves, review it in minutes, and make a decision. The value is not just speed—it is autonomy and reduced dependency.

Now consider a call center supervisor. Before, they may have manually tracked performance metrics, escalated issues late, and reacted after the fact. In the after state, alerts surface automatically, trends are visible in real time, and interventions happen earlier. The supervisor's work is different, even if the job title hasn't changed.[2]

These examples illustrate the point: The after state is defined by behavior, not history. We care about what actions are taken, how often, and by whom—now.

When the after state is clearly articulated, it becomes much easier to measure effort, frequency, and impact. It also prevents inflated claims that rely on vague comparisons to the past.

The after state is not an aspiration.

It is reality, captured cleanly.

Separating technology from behavior change

One of the most common sources of confusion in value discussions is the tendency to describe *how* work is done rather than *what* work is done. Technology changes are often mistaken for value changes when, in reality, they are only enablers.[3]

This framework is intentionally indifferent to technology choices.

We do not care whether someone uses System A or System B. We do not care if a task happens on Screen 1 or Screen 7. What we care about is whether the behavior associated with the work changed in a way that reduced effort, time, or friction.

For example, if someone used one system before and uses a different system now, that fact alone is irrelevant. If the effort required to perform the task stayed the same, there is no delta.

But if behavior changed, value emerges.

Consider a reporting scenario. Before, an analyst logged into five systems, extracted five datasets, spent five minutes per extract, and then spent another ten to fifteen minutes reconciling and aggregating the data. That is roughly forty minutes of effort per report.[4]

In the after state, the analyst logs into a single report where all data is already integrated, validated, and aggregated. They click once and receive an answer. No calculations. No transformations. No pivot tables.

The system changed, yes—but the value comes from the behavior change. Steps were eliminated. Cognitive load was reduced. Rework disappeared.

That is what we measure.

This distinction matters because technology-centric narratives often overstate value by assuming improvement simply because a new tool exists. Behavior-centric analysis avoids that trap. It forces specificity.

What did the person stop doing? What do they no longer need to think about? What actions are gone entirely?

When you separate technology from behavior, the after state becomes clearer, cleaner, and far more defensible.

Eliminating steps vs. compressing steps

Some processes are genuinely complex. Anyone who has ever sat through a 90-minute walkthrough of a manual workflow knows this pain. Conditional logic, exceptions, workarounds, and edge cases pile up over time, creating a spider web that feels impossible to untangle.

That complexity is not the problem.

The problem is trying to measure it at full resolution.

If a process has 29 steps, that level of detail may be useful for execution or system design, but it is not useful for value comparison. No stakeholder can hold 29 steps in their head and meaningfully compare before and after states.[5]

This is where compression becomes critical.

Not every step deserves equal treatment. Some steps consume meaningful time and effort. Others are trivial—clicks, notifications, or transitions that do not materially affect effort.

Your job is to distinguish between them.

Eliminate steps that do not consume effort or time from the value comparison. Then group the remaining steps into logical categories. Whether you do this manually or use AI as an accelerator, the goal is the same: Arrive at eight to 10 core steps.

Eight is a sweet spot. It provides enough specificity to be credible but not so much detail that the model becomes fragile. If someone challenges the omission of a detail, you can reasonably say, "That's part of step three."[6]

Compression does not mean hiding complexity. It means organizing it in a way that allows for clear comparison.

When before and after states are compressed consistently, deltas become visible and defensible.

Reducing handoffs and dependencies

A major objective of designing the after state is reducing net cycle time. That does not always mean reducing effort per task. Often, the biggest gains come from reducing waiting.

In many processes, work only takes minutes, but the process itself stretches across days or weeks. The culprit is almost always handoffs and dependencies.[7]

Every handoff introduces delay. Every dependency creates a potential bottleneck. When one team must wait for another, cycle time expands regardless of individual efficiency.

Designing the after state means intentionally reducing these friction points.

This may involve system automation, where inputs are provided automatically rather than manually. It may involve redesigning roles so fewer approvals are required. It may involve consolidating work so that fewer teams are involved end to end.[8]

These ideas align closely with Six Sigma and Lean principles, but you do not need formal terminology to apply them. The goal is simple: Reduce waste.

Waste shows up as waiting, rework, overprocessing, and unnecessary motion. The after state should systematically remove or reduce these wherever possible.

When handoffs decrease, cycle time shrinks. When dependencies are eliminated, flow improves. These changes often create more value than marginal efficiency gains within a single step.

Designing for flow is designing for impact.

Avoiding over-optimized future states

One of the biggest risks in defining the after state is optimism. It is tempting to describe a future where 20 steps become one and five weeks become 30 seconds. While that may sound impressive, it is rarely credible.[9]

Over-optimization undermines trust.

Stakeholders—especially finance leaders—have strong intuition for what is reasonable. When after-state assumptions feel too aggressive, scrutiny increases and the entire value narrative weakens.

The antidote is restraint.

Listen carefully to stakeholders and system experts. When you hear language that sounds overly optimistic, slow it down. Ask follow-up questions. Probe for edge cases, exceptions, and realities that temper the story.

A good test is this: Would a "normal person" believe this is reasonable? If the answer is no, adjust.

The goal is not to minimize value but to present value that survives challenge. Conservative, defensible after states almost always outperform aggressive, fragile ones in the long run.[10]

Credibility compounds.

Validating the after-state with operators

One of the most effective techniques for strengthening the after state is simple validation. Not formal sign-off. Not detailed time studies. Just directional confirmation from the people doing the work.

While defining the before state, I often ask a business partner or analyst a high-level question: "Are these roughly the eight steps you were doing before?" I avoid minutes, hours, or numbers. I focus on structure.[11]

Then, weeks later, I return to ask about the after state: "Based on our last conversation, it sounds like, with the new system in place, these six steps remain and these two were eliminated. Is that directionally accurate?"

This approach works because it respects expertise without overwhelming it.

You are not asking operators to validate calculations. You are asking them to validate reality.

If they nod and say, "Yes, that's basically how it works now," you have what you need. That acceptance becomes invaluable later when value is presented.

You do not need perfect precision at this stage. You need alignment.

When before and after states are directionally accepted by operators, the resulting value story becomes far harder to dispute.

That is how the after state moves from theoretical to trusted—and how quantified impact becomes credible impact.

CHAPTER 7

MEASURING THE DELTA

"Without continual growth and progress, such words as improvement, achievement and success have no meaning."

— BENJAMIN FRANKLIN

Effort avoided vs. effort reduced

One of the most important nuances in measuring delta is understanding the difference between effort avoided and effort reduced. The distinction may sound subtle, but it has significant implications for how value is calculated, communicated, and ultimately trusted.

Effort avoided means the work no longer happens at all. The step is gone. It has been eliminated, automated, or prevented entirely. No one performs it anymore. If a report is fully automated and nobody has to create it, validate it, or distribute it, that effort has been avoided. It does not recur. It does not consume time. It has effectively been removed from the system.[1]

Effort reduced, on the other hand, still exists. The step is still performed, but it takes less time, less effort, or less cognitive load. A task that once took five hours may now take two. A review meeting that lasted an hour may now last 30 minutes. A process that involved eight spreadsheets may now involve three.

Both matter—but they are not the same.

Effort avoided is usually higher-impact because it removes recurring work entirely. It simplifies the process and reduces ongoing operational burden. Effort reduced still creates value, but it must be counted carefully, because the effort has not gone to zero.[2]

This is where many value calculations quietly overstate impact. A stakeholder may say, “We don’t really do that anymore,” when in reality the step still takes 15 minutes instead of an hour. That 15 minutes still counts.

The framework forces precision here. Did the step disappear, or did it shrink?

Automation is often a mix of both. A report may no longer need to be manually compiled, but someone may still review it. A validation step may be lighter but not eliminated. Those nuances must be captured accurately.

Being explicit about effort avoided versus effort reduced strengthens credibility. It also makes later conversations with finance far easier, because the logic aligns with how operational work actually changes.

Clarity here prevents inflated deltas and builds trust in the numbers that follow.

Time saved vs. cycle time compressed

Another pair of terms that frequently get confused is time saved versus cycle time compressed. They are related, but they measure different dimensions of improvement—and conflating them weakens the analysis.

Time saved refers to labor. It is about effort. If a task drops from two hours to one hour, one hour of effort has been reduced or avoided. That hour can be translated into cost using a blended rate. This is the most straightforward form of delta.

Cycle time compression, however, is about throughput and speed. It measures how long a process takes from start to finish, regardless of how much labor is involved at each step.

A process may still require three hours of total effort, but if it used to span 10 days and now completes in six, the cycle time has been compressed by four days. No labor was eliminated—but the business moves faster.[3]

That distinction matters.

Cycle time improvements often unlock value indirectly. Faster processes can improve decision-making, reduce risk, increase responsiveness, and enable scale. These benefits may not immediately show up as cost avoided, but they are still real and measurable.

The mistake is treating cycle time compression as labor savings. They are not interchangeable. A compressed cycle does not necessarily mean hours were eliminated.

Both should be measured—but separately.

Effort reductions translate into cost. Cycle time compression translates into speed, capacity, and sometimes revenue acceleration. Keeping these measures distinct preserves analytical integrity and prevents double-counting.

Strong delta measurement recognizes that value is multidimensional—and treats each dimension with precision.

Cost avoided vs. cost eliminated

Cost avoided and cost eliminated are often used interchangeably, but they represent fundamentally different outcomes. Understanding the distinction is critical to maintaining credibility.

Cost eliminated is straightforward. A subscription is canceled. A contract ends. A line item disappears from the budget. The cost is visibly removed from the P&L. It is easy to audit and easy to verify.[4]

Cost avoided is more subtle—and more common in this framework.

Cost avoided means the spend never occurs because of a change. It is preventive. If automation allows a team to absorb growth without hiring two additional people, the salaries that were never added are costs avoided. They do not appear as reductions, but they are real.

Most operational improvements result in cost avoided, not cost eliminated. That does not make them less valuable—but it does require careful framing.

This framework intentionally focuses on cost avoided, because that is where most practitioner-driven value lives. The key is being explicit that avoided costs may not show up as immediate budget reductions.

When communicated clearly, cost avoided is defensible. When overstated or mischaracterized, it invites skepticism.

Precision in language preserves trust.

Translating deltas into hours and dollars

Most deltas start life as hours. Ten hours down to five. Two thousand five hundred hours down to 1,000. Those differences are meaningful, but they become far more powerful when translated into dollars.

This is where blended rates matter.

A blended rate is not just salary. It includes wages, benefits, payroll taxes, bonuses, healthcare, retirement contributions, facilities, IT tools, and shared services. It reflects the true cost of an hour of work.[5]

For many operational roles, a reasonable blended rate is around $75 per hour. For advanced technical or IT roles, $150 per hour is common. These are benchmarks, not absolutes, but they provide consistency.

Using blended rates avoids underestimating value and aligns the calculation with how finance views cost.[6]

Hours × blended rate = cost avoided.

Simple. Defensible. Repeatable.

Handling partial adoption and exceptions

Rarely does adoption happen exactly as planned. You may model 250 users and get 75. You may expect full rollout in one quarter and get it in three.

This does not invalidate the value—but it does change the timing.

A practical approach is to calculate a one-year cost avoided and a three-year cost avoided. The one-year view reflects reality. The three-year view shows scale.[7]

Both are useful—as long as adoption assumptions are explicit.

If adoption lags, near-term value should be adjusted downward. Long-term value can still be shown but clearly labeled.

Transparency here preserves trust and prevents accusations of overstatement.

Stress-testing delta assumptions

Measuring delta is not just analytical—it is personal. These numbers affect performance reviews, compensation, promotions, and funding decisions. That makes them sensitive.[8]

Because of that, stress-testing assumptions is not optional.

Ask yourself: Would a reasonable CFO believe this? Would a controller pressure-test it and still nod?

Sometimes that means dialing numbers back, even if the original estimate is defensible. Plausibility matters as much as precision.

I've seen situations where a 1% revenue lift translated into $150 million in value. The math was sound—but the number felt implausible. Reducing the assumption to 0.25% preserved credibility while still supporting the decision.[9]

The goal is not maximum value.

The goal is believable value.

When deltas survive stress-testing, they empower teams instead of exposing them.

That is how quantified impact becomes sustainable impact.

CHAPTER 8

ANNUALIZING AND SCALING VALUE

"Small daily improvements over time lead to stunning results."

— ROBIN SHARMA

From task-level savings to weekly impact

On average, knowledge workers lose between 20–30% of their week to low-value, repeatable tasks. Individually, those tasks feel insignificant. Collectively, they quietly consume entire days of organizational capacity.[1]

That's why task-level savings are both powerful and dangerous. Powerful because they are concrete and observable. Dangerous because, if left at the task level, they feel trivial and easy to dismiss.

The first step in scaling impact is recognizing that no meaningful initiative starts big. It starts with a task. A report that takes 10 minutes less. A review that no longer happens. A manual lookup that disappears. These are the atomic units of value.

On their own, 10 minutes saved doesn't sound impressive. But tasks do not exist in isolation. They recur. Daily. Weekly. Sometimes dozens of times per week across a team. The moment you apply frequency, the math changes.[2]

Ten minutes saved, five times a week, is nearly an hour. Multiply that across 10 people, and you've freed an entire workday every week. That is no longer a rounding error—it is capacity.

Weekly framing matters because it matches how work is experienced. People plan weeks, not years. Leaders feel pressure weekly. Bottlenecks show up weekly. When you translate task-level deltas into weekly impact, the value becomes tangible.

This also prevents exaggeration. Weekly rollups are grounded. They are close enough to reality that stakeholders can sanity-check them against lived experience. "Yes, that feels right" is a powerful validation.

Think of it like fuel efficiency. Saving a few cents per mile doesn't feel impactful—until you realize the fleet drives millions of miles a year. The mileage didn't change dramatically; the repetition did the work.

Task-level savings become real when time is allowed to do what it always does: repeat.

Small deltas don't lack value—they lack context.

Monthly, quarterly, and annual rollups

A single process improvement rarely changes the business. What changes the business is sustained impact over time. That's why rollups matter.

A monthly rollup introduces rhythm. It captures enough repetition to smooth out anomalies without drifting into abstraction. Monthly views answer the question: Is this improvement part of how we operate now, or was it a one-off?[3]

Quarterly rollups introduce credibility. Most organizations plan, review, and course-correct quarterly. When value aligns with that cadence, it enters leadership conversations naturally. It stops being "project value" and starts becoming "operational performance."

Annual rollups do something different. They shift the narrative from improvement to contribution. At that scale, value is no longer about effort saved—it's about capacity created, risk reduced, and speed enabled across the business.[4]

The mistake many practitioners make is jumping straight to annual numbers. Annualized value without intermediate grounding feels speculative, even when the math is sound. Monthly and quarterly rollups act as steppingstones that make annual figures believable.

Each rollup serves a different purpose. Monthly shows consistency. Quarterly shows momentum. Annual shows magnitude.

Used together, they tell a coherent story: This improvement works, it lasts, and it matters.

Consider revenue reporting. Daily sales numbers are noisy. Weekly trends provide signal. Quarterly performance drives decisions. Annual results shape strategy. Value behaves the same way.

When rollups align with how leaders already think, they stop questioning the math and start asking how to do more.

Value becomes strategic when it speaks the language of time.

Scaling by users, teams, and regions

One of the fastest ways to undermine credibility is to scale value too aggressively, too quickly. One of the fastest ways to undersell impact is not to scale at all.

Scaling is not multiplication—it's translation.

The first layer is users. If a process improvement works for one person, does it work the same way for 10? Are their roles similar? Is their usage frequency comparable? Scaling at the user level requires sameness.

The second layer is teams. Teams introduce variation—different workflows, priorities, and constraints. Scaling across teams requires validation, not assumption. The question becomes: Does this change remove the same effort, or does it simply shift it?[5]

The third layer is regions. Regions introduce complexity—regulatory differences, time zones, local practices. Value often scales unevenly here, and that's okay. Precision matters more than symmetry.

The key is progressive scaling. Prove value at one layer before moving to the next. Each expansion should be earned, not assumed.

This is similar to franchising. A restaurant that works in one city doesn't automatically work in 50. You standardize what matters, adapt what doesn't, and grow deliberately.

When scaling is done responsibly, value compounds naturally. When it's rushed, it collapses under scrutiny.

Scale doesn't amplify value—it tests it.

One-year vs. three-year value horizons

Most organizations think in one-year increments, but real impact often unfolds over longer horizons. That tension creates confusion when presenting value.

A one-year horizon answers the question: What did this change deliver in reality? It reflects adoption delays, learning curves, and operational friction. It is conservative by nature—and that's a strength.

A three-year horizon answers a different question: What does this improvement enable once it's fully embedded? It shows the structural value of the change, not just the initial results.[6]

Both views are valid. The mistake is treating them as interchangeable.

One-year value builds trust. Three-year value builds ambition. Presented together, they show both discipline and vision.

Think of it like building a bridge. The first year proves it stands. The next three show how much traffic it can support.

When horizons are clearly labeled and logically connected, stakeholders stop arguing about timelines and start discussing priorities.[7]

Time horizons don't inflate value—they reveal its shape.

When (and when not) to project growth

Roughly 70% of large-scale performance forecasts fail not because the underlying work didn't deliver value but because growth assumptions were layered on top without structural support. In other words, the improvement worked—but the projection didn't.[8]

This is why growth is the most misunderstood and misused element of scaled value.

Growth projections are seductive because they turn solid operational improvements into headline numbers. A process that saves one hour today suddenly saves 10,000 hours tomorrow—on paper. The problem is that growth only materializes when something forces or enables it to materialize.

The first question to ask before projecting growth is simple: What actually changes over time? If nothing about the system, usage, volume, or reach changes, growth is not a projection—it is repetition. Repetition is fine, but it should be labeled honestly as steady-state value.

Growth becomes legitimate when one of three things is true: Usage expands because more people are required to use the capability. Volume increases because demand grows independent of the improvement. Or scope widens because the solution is intentionally rolled out to new areas. Without one of these drivers, growth is narrative, not analysis.[9]

Another trap is confusing adoption with growth. Adoption curves are real, but they are finite. Once adoption stabilizes, value stabilizes, too. Extending an adoption curve indefinitely creates inflated numbers that fail basic scrutiny.

There are also moments when not projecting growth is the most credible choice. If volumes are volatile, if adoption is uncertain, or if organizational change is still underway, conservative framing protects trust. You can always revise upward later. You rarely recover credibility once it's lost.

A useful way to think about growth is manufacturing capacity. A machine that produces 100 units per day will not magically produce 200 unless you increase shifts, speed, or demand. Efficiency alone doesn't create growth—constraints do.

The strongest value stories separate realized value, enabled value, and hypothetical value. They do not blend them.

Growth is not a multiplier you apply.

It is a consequence you earn.

Real growth doesn't come from better math—it comes from changed constraints.

Presenting scaled value responsibly

Executives make decisions in minutes, but value stories live or die on seconds. Studies consistently show that when numbers feel unclear or overstated, trust erodes immediately—even if the underlying analysis is sound. Presentation is not cosmetic; it is structural.[10]

Responsible presentation starts with separation: What is actual. What is projected. What is conditional. When these blur together, skepticism fills the gap. When they are clearly labeled, confidence grows.

One of the most effective techniques is to anchor the conversation in what undeniably happened: "Here is what changed. Here is what no longer occurs. Here is the effort that was avoided." This grounds the audience before any scaling enters the discussion.

From there, scaled value should be introduced as a logical extension, not a leap. Each expansion should answer an implicit question: Why is it reasonable to believe this repeats, spreads, or persists? If that question is not answered, the number will be challenged—even if no one says so out loud.[11]

Responsible presentation also avoids precision theater. Overly exact figures imply certainty that does not exist. Rounded numbers, ranges, and directional language often increase credibility because they acknowledge variability rather than denying it.

Another overlooked element is empathy. Finance leaders, controllers, and executives are not trying to "kill" value stories—they are trying to protect decision quality. When value is framed transparently, with visible assumptions and trade-offs, it becomes a decision aid rather than a sales pitch.

A helpful analogy is forecasting weather for a business trip. You don't present a single temperature and declare certainty. You describe likely conditions, ranges, and risks. That framing helps people prepare, not argue.

The goal of presenting scaled value responsibly is not to win approval—it is to invite confidence. When stakeholders trust the framing, they engage with the implications instead of debating the arithmetic.

The paradox is that the more honest the presentation, the more influential it becomes.

Value earns influence not by being impressive, but by being believable.

CHAPTER 9

WHAT MAKES A VALUE CLAIM DEFENSIBLE

"In God we trust; all others must bring data."

— W. EDWARDS DEMING

Assumptions that matter—and those that don't

When value claims fall apart under scrutiny, it is rarely because the math is wrong. More often, it's because the wrong assumptions were treated as important—or the important ones were buried among noise.

A defensible value claim starts with discernment. You must be able to separate assumptions that materially influence the delta from those that are largely irrelevant. Not all assumptions deserve equal airtime.

For example, where someone performs an activity usually does not matter. Whether a task is completed in California or Ireland does not, by itself, change the value equation. Geography may affect rates later, but the location alone does not create or destroy value.

What does matter is effort. If one person completes a task in one hour and another takes five, that difference is meaningful. It directly drives effort avoided, cost avoided, and, sometimes, cycle time compression. That assumption belongs front and center.[1]

Another category of low-impact assumptions includes activities outside the scope of the process being changed. Many organizations have deeply inefficient processes that are adjacent to, but not part of, the initiative being measured. While those inefficiencies may be real—and frustrating—they are irrelevant if they are not impacted by the change.

Including them weakens the value story rather than strengthening it.

The litmus test is simple: Does this assumption directly affect effort avoided, cost avoided, cycle time reduction, or revenue uplift? If the answer is no, it is not a critical assumption for the value claim.[2]

That does not mean you ignore everything else. Context can be captured separately for understanding, but defensible value claims remain focused. Precision beats comprehensiveness.

Strong value practitioners are ruthless editors. They know that every assumption included invites scrutiny. By limiting assumptions to those that actually move the delta, you make the value easier to defend, easier to explain, and harder to dismantle.

Defensibility is not about saying more.

It's about saying what matters.

Choosing credible labor and cost rates

Few things destroy credibility faster than implausible labor rates. You can have a perfectly sound process delta, but if the rate applied to it feels wrong, the entire value claim becomes suspect.

The first rule is simple: Use real roles. "Call center representative," "business analyst," "senior developer"—these must map to actual job titles or recognizable equivalents within the organization. Invented or overly abstract roles raise immediate red flags.

The second rule is alignment. Rates must reflect how your organization actually sources labor. If a call center operates offshore in Manila under a fixed-price contract, applying a $150 U.S. blended rate is indefensible, no matter how convenient it is.[3]

Similarly, if expert development work is consistently performed onshore by senior engineers, applying a low offshore benchmark understates value and misrepresents reality.

But they must still be grounded in organizational truth. Industry benchmarks are useful only when they resemble your operating model.

When in doubt, involve finance. Asking, "What is a reasonable blended rate for this role in this location?" does two things. It improves accuracy, and it creates shared ownership of the assumptions.

Credible rates don't need to be perfect. They need to be believable.

Executives have a strong intuition for what "sounds right." If your rates trigger disbelief, no amount of explanation will save the value claim.

Defensible value is not about maximizing dollars.

It's about earning trust in the math.

Documenting sources and constraints

Value claims are not challenged if they will be pressure tested—they are challenged. Defensibility depends on being prepared before the question is asked.

That preparation starts with sources.

Every meaningful input—process steps, effort estimates, frequencies—should trace back to a real conversation with a real person. Ideally, a business analyst, operator, or subject-matter expert who actually performs the work.

You do not need perfect precision. Estimates are acceptable. What matters is that someone credible can say, "Yes, that's directionally accurate."

Document who provided what. Not for formality, but for resilience.

The same applies to constraints. Rates, staffing models, sourcing decisions, regulatory requirements—these all shape what is possible. When constraints are acknowledged upfront, they prevent later derailment.[4]

Finance is a particularly important partner here. Asking finance for guidance on blended rates or cost structures creates a paper trail and establishes boundaries that protect the analysis.[5]

Documentation does not need to be heavy. It needs to be accessible. When someone asks, "Where did that number come from?" you should be able to answer calmly and clearly.

Defensibility lives in readiness.

Confidence levels and sensitivity ranges

There is a persistent myth that value claims must be presented as a single precise number to be credible. In reality, precision without context often reduces trust.

Confidence levels and sensitivity ranges acknowledge uncertainty without undermining value.

It is perfectly acceptable to say, "At 50% adoption, this delivers roughly $15,000 annually; at full adoption, closer to $30,000." That framing is honest and informative.

Similarly, expressing confidence—"We are 90–95% confident in this range"—signals rigor rather than weakness. It shows you understand where assumptions are conservative and where variability exists.

Sensitivity ranges are especially powerful when rates or adoption levels are debated. They allow stakeholders to explore scenarios without attacking the core logic.[6]

The key is consistency. Ranges should be grounded in the same assumptions as the base case, not invented to soften scrutiny.

Strong value claims don't pretend to be exact.

They are transparent about what could change—and why.

Auditability and traceability

Nothing derails a value conversation faster than an untraceable number. One question—"Where did that six hours come from?"—can hijack an entire meeting.

Auditability means every number has a lineage. Traceability means you can explain that lineage quickly.

If someone asks where a number came from, the answer should not be defensive. It should be factual. "That estimate came from a conversation with Michelle in October, who performs that step weekly."[7]

That level of traceability does not require exhaustive documentation. It requires discipline. Notes. Names. Dates. Context.

Auditability is not about inviting audits—it's about surviving them.

When traceability exists, you can redirect the conversation back to value instead of chasing details.[8]

Preparedness keeps control.

Defending numbers in executive reviews

The most effective way to defend numbers is to reduce the need to defend them at all.

Preemptive transparency is powerful. Appendices that list contributors, assumptions, roles, and process boundaries demonstrate mastery before questions arise.

When executives see familiar names—"Oh, Dave was involved"—confidence increases immediately. Social validation matters.[9]

Defending numbers is less about argument and more about presence. When you clearly understand the process, the people, and the assumptions, that confidence is felt.[10]

Executives rarely attack well-understood numbers. They attack ambiguity.

A defensible value claim signals competence, preparation, and respect for the audience's time.

And when those signals are present, the conversation shifts from "Is this real?" to "What do we do next?"

PART III

THE WORKBOOK: REAL EXAMPLES, REAL NUMBERS

Part III is where the framework stops being an idea and starts behaving like an instrument.

In Part II, we built the Quantified Impact Framework™ as a shared logic: Define "before," define "after," measure the delta, scale it, and translate it into business language. That structure matters—but structure alone can still feel theoretical until you see it applied to work that looks like your work.

This section is the workbook. Real examples. Real numbers. Real constraints. Not polished case studies engineered to "win" a value story but the kind of messy, operational reality most teams live in: manual master data mediation, decision cycles slowed by waiting and reconciliation, supply chains operating without early visibility, analytics delivered as one-off projects instead of reusable capabilities, migrations that stall progress, cloud spend that grows without discipline, and legacy systems kept alive "just in case."

Each chapter follows the same pattern. We locate the friction in the current operating model, define the before and after states at the process level, and quantify what changed—hours avoided, cycle time compressed, spend avoided, risk reduced, throughput increased. Then we scale responsibly, separating what is realized from what is enabled.

As you move through these examples, you'll start to see something else emerge: reusable value patterns—flow, awareness, signal extraction, guardrails, durable assets. These are not one-time wins. They are repeatable capabilities.

The goal here isn't inspiration.

It's replication.

CHAPTER 10

ELIMINATING MANUAL MASTER DATA MANAGEMENT

(REPLACING HUMAN BOTTLENECKS WITH SYSTEMIC FLOW)

"All we are doing is looking at the time line, from the moment the customer gives us an order to the point when we collect the cash. And we are reducing that time line by reducing the non-value-added wastes."

— TAIICHI OHNO

Where human mediation breaks system flow

Most organizations believe their master data problems are governance problems.

They respond with policies, approval layers, and specialized roles designed to "control" data creation and change. On paper, this looks responsible. In practice, it quietly undermines the very systems those controls are meant to protect.

System flow depends on continuity. Transactions must move from intent to execution without unnecessary interruption. When humans are placed directly in the path of routine, high-frequency work, the system no longer flows—it waits. Over time, waiting becomes normalized. Queues become invisible. Delays are explained away as "process."[1]

This is not a failure of people. It is a failure of design.

Master data sits at the center of enterprise operations. When it is mediated manually, every downstream system inherits that friction. Reporting lags. Reconciliation increases. Trust erodes. What looks like a localized operational choice becomes an enterprise-wide constraint.

To understand why this happens—and why it persists—we must start by examining the before state with precision: who was involved, how work moved, and where flow was broken by human intervention.[2]

[FRAMEWORK STEPS: BEFORE STATE, ACTORS]

In many enterprises, master data is treated as a control problem instead of a flow problem.

In this example, core reference entities—products, customers, and commercial attributes—were created and maintained through a human-mediated process spanning multiple systems. While governance existed, execution relied on a small group of specialists acting as the connective tissue between platforms.

Before State Defined

- Master data requests submitted via ticket or email
- Specialists manually validated, keyed, and re-keyed data
- Downstream systems consumed updates asynchronously
- Errors surfaced late, often during reporting or reconciliation

Actors Identified

- Business requestors (Sales, Finance, Operations)
- Master Data Specialists
- Reporting / Analytics teams
- Application support (escalations)

Humans were not supervising the system.

They were the system.

This created a structural bottleneck: Throughput was constrained by people, not demand.

The critical insight from this before state is not that people made mistakes or moved slowly. It is that the organization unknowingly converted a system problem into a staffing problem.

Once humans became the connective tissue between systems, throughput could only scale linearly—and only at the cost of more effort, more coordination, and more delay. Every additional request increased pressure on the same constrained group. The system did not fail loudly. It degraded quietly.

This is how structural bottlenecks hide in plain sight.

When humans are the system, improvement efforts gravitate toward training, prioritization, and heroics. None of those restore flow. They simply help people cope with its absence.

By clearly defining the before state and identifying the actors involved, we surface the real constraint: not governance, not tools, but where mediation sits in the transaction path. Only by moving that mediation out of the critical flow can the system begin to operate as a system again.

The cost of paused systems and queued work

Queues feel harmless because they are familiar. Every organization has them. Requests waiting in inboxes. Tickets aging in systems. Work paused until someone has time to act.[3]

What is rarely examined is the systemic cost of those pauses.

When a transaction stops moving, the system is not idle—it is accumulating hidden debt. Downstream processes stall. Parallel work proceeds with incomplete or outdated information. Errors are not prevented; they are deferred.

Manual master data processes are particularly prone to this pattern because the work feels episodic rather than continuous. Each request appears small. Each delay seems tolerable. Yet when multiplied across days, weeks, and years, these micro-pauses become a material operational cost.[4]

To make that cost visible, we must map the process as it actually runs and measure how often it occurs. Frequency is what transforms inconvenience into impact. Without it, queued work remains anecdotal. With it, the economics of paused systems become undeniable.

(FRAMEWORK STEPS: PROCESS STEPS, FREQUENCY)

Before-State Process (Mapped)

1. Request submitted
2. Manual validation against policy
3. Entry into primary system
4. Manual replication or transformation for secondary systems
5. Downstream reconciliation when mismatches appeared

Frequency Captured (Assumption—Explicit)

- Average requests per day: 12
- Operating days per year: 240
- Annual transactions: 2,880

Each transaction paused system flow until a human completed the handoff.

This is the hidden cost of queued work: Systems wait while people catch up.

Once frequency is applied, the nature of the problem changes. What appeared to be a modest administrative burden reveals itself as a persistent drag on system throughput.

Each transaction waited its turn. Each handoff required attention. Each pause compounded the time before data could be trusted downstream. The system was not slow because it was complex. It was slow because it was designed to stop.

This is the hidden tax of human-mediated flow: The organization pays in elapsed time, rework, and attention long before it pays in dollars. And because the pauses are distributed, no single delay feels urgent enough to fix.

By explicitly mapping steps and capturing frequency, the organization converts intuition into evidence. Queues stop being background noise and become quantifiable constraints. This creates the conditions for a different question—not "How do we process requests faster?" but "Why are we stopping the system at all?"

Designing for flow instead of control

When organizations recognize the cost of manual mediation, their first instinct is often to automate approvals rather than redesign flow. This preserves the underlying assumption: that control must sit in the middle of the transaction.

Flow-based design starts from a different premise.

Instead of asking who should approve each action, it asks where rules belong, where variability actually occurs, and how exceptions differ from the norm. In high-volume systems, most transactions are predictable. Designing as if every case is exceptional guarantees unnecessary friction.[5]

Shifting from control to flow does not mean abandoning governance. It means embedding it where it can operate continuously and consistently—inside the system itself.

This requires a deliberate after-state definition. Not a tool swap. Not a workflow tweak. A structural change in how data enters, moves through, and exits the enterprise.

[FRAMEWORK STEPS: AFTER STATE]

The organization reframed master data as a transactional flow, not an approval workflow.

After State Defined

- A centralized reference data service became the system of record
- Validation rules embedded at ingestion
- Downstream systems subscribed to changes automatically
- Humans handled exceptions, not every transaction

Control did not disappear. It moved upstream and into the system.

The after state reframes the role of both systems and people. Systems handle what they do best: enforcing rules at scale, propagating change instantly, and maintaining consistency across consumers. Humans handle what they do best: judgment, ambiguity, and true exceptions.

Control becomes preventive instead of reactive. Errors are stopped at ingestion rather than discovered downstream. Flow becomes the default condition, not something to be earned through effort.

This design choice has a compounding effect. As volume grows, the system absorbs it without additional coordination. As complexity increases, rules evolve without adding handoffs.

Designing for flow is not an optimization. It is an architectural stance. Once taken, it fundamentally alters how work scales—and how value is created—across the organization.

Shifting effort from repetition to exception handling

Automation discussions often fixate on elimination: removing work, reducing roles, cutting cost. That framing misses the more important shift—where human effort is applied.

In manual master data environments, effort is consumed by repetition. Skilled people spend their time validating, copying, correcting, and reconciling information that rarely deviates from known patterns. Their judgment is underutilized precisely because it is needed everywhere.

A flow-based design inverts this equation.

By measuring effort per transaction before and after, we can see not just time saved but effort reallocated. This distinction matters. It explains why organizations feel relief after redesign even when headcount remains constant.

The value is not that humans disappear. It is that they finally work where humans add value.

[FRAMEWORK STEPS: EFFORT PER STEP, DELTA CALCULATION BEGINS]

Effort per Transaction (Before)

- Manual handling time: 30 minutes per request
- Validation
- Entry
- Follow-up
- Corrections

Effort per Transaction (After)

- Automated handling for standard cases
- Human review required for ~10% of transactions
- Average human effort per transaction (blended): 5 minutes

Effort Delta (Per Transaction)

- Before: 30 minutes
- After: 5 minutes
- Net savings: 25 minutes

This is the critical shift: Effort moves from repetition to judgment.

The delta in effort per transaction is the mechanical heart of this chapter. It is where abstraction becomes arithmetic.

Reducing human involvement from every transaction to a small exception set changes the economics of work. Time is no longer fragmented across thousands of low-value touches. Attention is no longer diluted. Quality improves because people are no longer exhausted by repetition.

This shift also changes risk. When humans only intervene where judgment is required, their decisions matter more—and errors matter less because they are rarer and more visible.

Effort has not been eliminated. It has been concentrated. That concentration is what makes scale possible without proportional cost.

Flow at scale and compounding transaction cost

Improvements that matter once do not matter much. Improvements that repeat quietly, thousands of times per year, reshape economics.

This is where flow design separates itself from one-time efficiency projects. By scaling effort savings across real transaction volumes and applying a blended rate, we expose the compounding nature of manual mediation.[6]

The math here is intentionally simple. Complexity obscures impact. The goal is not precision to the dollar but clarity about magnitude.

When flow improves, savings recur automatically. No retraining. No renegotiation. No renewed initiative. The system simply keeps moving.

(FRAMEWORK STEPS: SCALE, BLENDED RATE, MATH SHOWN ONCE)

Now we scale the improvement.

Annual Effort Avoided

- Transactions per year: 2,880
- Minutes saved per transaction: 25
- Total minutes avoided: 72,000
- Total hours avoided: 1,200

Blended Rate (Assumption – Explicit)

- Blended fully loaded rate: $75/hour
  (mix of data specialists, analysts, and support)

Annualized Value (Math shown once)
1,200 hours × $75/hour = $90,000 per year

$90,000 cost avoided Year 1
$270,000 cost avoided Year 3

This is only the direct labor component.
It does not include:

- Downstream reconciliation avoided
- Faster availability of new entities
- Reduced reporting disputes

Those are real but excluded to remain conservative.

The conservative framing matters. Even when excluding downstream effects, the value is material and persistent. And because it is structural, it does not erode over time.

This is how organizations create capacity without budgeting for it. The system absorbs growth without demanding more people to manage it.

As transaction volumes rise, the avoided cost rises with them. This is the opposite of manual mediation, where growth increases strain and risk.

Flow does not just save money. It changes how cost behaves under scale.

The flow pattern as a reusable capability

Patterns matter because they travel.

What makes this example powerful is not the specific systems involved but the structure of the problem and the shape of the solution: High-frequency transactions. Human mediation. Invisible queues. Compounding cost.

These conditions exist everywhere in the enterprise—far beyond master data.

By abstracting the pattern, organizations gain a reusable lens for identifying where value is trapped by design rather than performance.[7]

[FRAMEWORK STEP: TRANSLATE INTO BUSINESS LANGUAGE]

This example demonstrates a reusable enterprise pattern:

When humans sit in the middle of high-frequency transactions, the organization pays a compounding tax on growth.

By replacing human mediation with systemic flow:

- Throughput scales without headcount
- Quality improves as a byproduct
- Cost per transaction collapses over time

BUSINESS TRANSLATION

This is not an IT efficiency story.

It is:

- Capacity creation without hiring
- Cost avoidance as volume grows
- Risk reduction through consistency

Most importantly, it is structural.

Once flow is designed into the system, the value recurs every year.

The ultimate value of flow design is durability.

Once embedded, it does not rely on discipline, attention, or enforcement. It simply operates. Year after year, it delivers capacity, consistency, and cost avoidance without requiring renewed justification.[8]

This is why flow is strategic. It converts operational improvements into enduring advantage.

The organization is no longer paying a tax on its own growth. It is compounding returns instead.

And that is the difference between fixing a process and redesigning a system.

Tying it all together

The chapters in this book focus on patterns, not projects. But patterns only matter if they can be translated into defensible business value.

The following example shows how one of these patterns is captured using a standard business value framework—moving from the business problem, through the solution, to a quantified outcome.

This is not a hypothetical case; it is a practical illustration of how impact can be articulated clearly, consistently, and credibly using real operating assumptions.

1. TITLE

Automating Core Reference Data to Remove Manual Throughput Constraints

2. CURRENT SITUATION

(In business terms, what was the gap or the need?)

Core reference data (product identifiers, attributes, and classifications) was maintained through a human-mediated process spanning multiple systems. Requests were routed through a small group of specialists responsible for validation, entry, and downstream synchronization.

While governance controls existed, execution depended on manual handoffs. As transaction volume increased, this created a structural bottleneck:

- Requests queued behind limited specialist capacity
- Updates propagated inconsistently across systems
- Errors surfaced late, often during reporting or reconciliation
- Business teams experienced delays unrelated to actual system capability

The gap was not policy or tooling. It was that humans were embedded directly in high-frequency data flow.

3. OBJECTIVE

(In business terms, what was the business trying to solve?)

The business objective was to increase master data throughput and reliability **without adding headcount** while maintaining governance and reducing downstream rework.

Specifically, the organization aimed to:

- Eliminate manual handling for standard master data changes
- Reduce cycle time from request to availability
- Shift human effort from repetitive entry to exception management
- Create a scalable model where volume growth did not increase operating cost

4. SOLUTION

(What was the solution, and how did analytics products/services assist?)

A centralized reference data service was implemented as the system of record, with analytics-enabled validation embedded at ingestion.

Key elements of the solution included:

- Standardized data definitions and validation rules enforced programmatically
- Automated propagation of approved changes to downstream consumers
- Analytics-driven monitoring to surface exceptions and anomalies
- Human review applied only to non-standard or failed transactions

Analytics products supported this shift by making data quality measurable at the point of entry, rather than after consumption.

5. BUSINESS VALUE

(Describe the business value in VERY SPECIFIC terms.)

This initiative removed humans from the critical path of routine master data transactions.

As a result:

- The majority of master data updates flowed end-to-end without manual intervention
- Specialist effort previously spent on repetitive entry and reconciliation was eliminated
- Data became available faster and more consistently across consuming systems
- Downstream reporting corrections and clarification cycles were reduced

The most important outcome was structural:
Throughput scaled with demand, not with staffing.

6. BUSINESS VALUE CALCULATION DETAILS

(Describe in very specific terms HOW the business value was calculated.)

To quantify value, the organization compared effort per transaction before and after automation.

Assumptions (Conservative):

- Average master data transactions per year: ~2,500
- Manual handling time before automation: ~25 minutes per transaction
- Residual human review after automation: ~5 minutes per transaction (exceptions only)

Effort Delta per Transaction:

- 25 minutes (before) – 5 minutes (after) = 20 minutes saved

Annual Effort Avoided:

- 2,500 transactions × 20 minutes = 50,000 minutes
- 50,000 minutes ÷ 60 = ~833 hours per year

Blended Fully Loaded Rate:

- Data specialists and analyst roles: ~$95/hour

7. TOTAL AMOUNT OF VALUE FOR THE YEAR (IN $)

833 hours × $95/hour = ~$79,000 per year

$79,000 cost avoided Year 1
$237,000 cost avoided Year 3

This figure reflects direct labor capacity created through automation.

It intentionally excludes:

- Faster product or customer onboarding
- Reduced downstream reporting corrections
- Improved trust in reference data

Those benefits exist but were not monetized to keep the estimate conservative.

CHAPTER 11

FROM WAITING TO KNOWING: COLLAPSING DECISION CYCLES

"Do not wait to strike till the iron is hot; but make it hot by striking."

— WILLIAM BUTLER YEATS

Decision latency as an invisible operational tax

Most organizations believe slow decisions are a leadership problem. When outcomes lag, the explanation defaults to alignment, hesitation, or risk aversion. Yet in many cases, leaders are ready to decide—they simply do not have validated information soon enough to act.[1]

This distinction matters because it shifts responsibility from individuals to systems.

Decision latency is rarely visible on a balance sheet. It does not appear as a line item. Instead, it manifests as drift: missed windows, delayed corrections, and growing dependence on experience over evidence. Over time, this becomes normalized. Reviews slide. Assumptions harden. Meetings focus on explanations rather than action.

At the root is not indecision but timing. When insight arrives days after reality has changed, even correct decisions lose value.

To understand this dynamic, we must define the before state precisely—not in terms of reporting tools but in terms of how long it takes for the organization to know what is happening. Only then can we see decision latency for what it is: an invisible operational tax paid repeatedly, often without recognition.[2]

[FRAMEWORK STEP 1: DEFINE BEFORE STATE]

In many organizations, decisions are not delayed because leaders hesitate. They are delayed because validated information arrives too late.

In this example, operational and commercial leaders depended on recurring performance views spanning sales, supply chain, and financial indicators. The questions were routine:

- Are we on plan this week?
- Where are we drifting?
- What changed since the last review?

The answers existed—but only after manual assembly, reconciliation, and validation.

This delay created an invisible operational tax:

- Decisions deferred
- Corrections applied later than optimal
- Growing reliance on intuition over evidence

The before state reveals a critical asymmetry: The organization generated data continuously but insight intermittently. That gap is where decision latency lives.

Nothing in this model prevented leaders from deciding. What prevented timely action was the delay between events and awareness. By the time answers were validated, the moment to intervene had often passed.

This is why decision latency is so difficult to address. It does not feel like a failure. It feels like the cost of doing business. Yet every deferral accumulates risk—not through inaction but through late action.

By defining this before state clearly, the organization surfaces a problem that is usually misdiagnosed. The issue is not leadership behavior. It is the system's inability to deliver trustworthy information at the pace the business actually moves.

MANUAL MECHANICS OF WAITING AND RECONCILIATION

Waiting rarely appears in process diagrams, yet it dominates real-world operations. Between extraction and validation, between discrepancy and resolution, work stalls—not because it is hard but because it is interdependent.

Manual reporting environments amplify this effect. Data arrives on different schedules. Definitions are aligned after aggregation. Validation happens only once numbers are already visible—and contested.

Each of these mechanics introduces delay. Individually, they seem reasonable. Collectively, they create a rhythm where decisions wait on reconciliation rather than reality.[3]

To make waiting visible, we must map not just what happens but who is involved and how often the cycle repeats. Frequency turns delay into cost. Actors turn abstraction into accountability.

Only then can we see how reconciliation, intended as a safeguard, becomes the primary source of latency.

(FRAMEWORK STEPS 3–5: PROCESS STEPS, ACTORS, FREQUENCY)

Actors Identified

- Reporting / BI Analysts
- Functional Managers
- Data Platform Support

Before-State Process (Mapped)

1. Data extracted manually from multiple systems
2. Files reconciled and adjusted in spreadsheets
3. Metrics recalculated and reviewed
4. Discrepancies resolved through analyst–stakeholder cycles
5. Final reports distributed for decision-making

Each step introduced **waiting**, not because of complexity but because:

- Data arrived at different times
- Definitions were enforced late
- Validation happened after aggregation

Frequency Captured (Explicit)

- Weekly operational reporting cycle
- Monthly executive rollups
- Ad hoc requests layered on top

Decisions waited until reconciliation completed.

This process map exposes a crucial truth: The organization was not slow because it lacked capability. It was slow because it validated too late.

Every reconciliation cycle pushed certainty further from the event itself. Each analyst–stakeholder loop extended the time-to-know, even as effort increased.

Because this happened on a predictable cadence, the delay became accepted. Decisions were scheduled around the process instead of the process serving decisions.

By naming the actors and capturing frequency, the organization converts vague frustration into structural understanding. Waiting is no longer incidental. It is designed into the flow.

And anything designed into the flow can be redesigned out of it.

Visibility as a system-level property

Most organizations treat visibility as an output: something produced at the end of a reporting process. In this model, insight is assembled, checked, and delivered—usually just in time for the next meeting.

A system-level view reframes visibility as a condition, not a deliverable.

When definitions, validation, and refresh logic are embedded upstream, insight no longer depends on orchestration. It exists continuously, available the moment a question is asked.

This shift is subtle but profound. It changes the role of analysts, the cadence of decisions, and the expectations of leaders. Instead of asking for reports, decision-makers interrogate reality directly.[4]

Defining the after state at this level makes it clear that the goal is not faster reporting. It is eliminating the concept of waiting for insight altogether.

[FRAMEWORK STEP 2: DEFINE AFTER STATE]

The organization reframed visibility as a **system property**, not a reporting task.

After State Defined (Anonymized)

- Standardized performance definitions embedded upstream
- Automated refresh and validation routines
- A shared performance layer accessible directly by decision-makers
- Analysts focused on interpretation, not assembly

Insight was no longer *produced* on demand.

It was continuously available.

In the after state, visibility ceases to be episodic. It becomes ambient.

Because definitions are enforced before aggregation, trust is established upstream. Because refresh is automated, timeliness is assumed. Because access is shared, interpretation replaces debate.

This does not reduce analytical rigor. It increases it. Analysts spend their time understanding movement rather than defending numbers.

By making visibility a system property, the organization collapses the distance between events and understanding. Insight is no longer produced. It is revealed.

Measuring time-to-know instead of time-to-build

Traditional reporting metrics focus on effort: hours spent building, validating, and distributing reports. While useful for staffing discussions, they miss the more important question: How long does it take for the organization to know something meaningful?[5]

Time-to-know reframes performance around outcomes rather than activity. It measures the gap between reality and awareness, not between task start and task completion.

This distinction matters because decisions do not wait for reports to be built. They wait for confidence.

By shifting the measurement lens, the organization aligns effort with purpose. The goal is no longer to produce artifacts efficiently but to minimize the delay between change and comprehension.

Only then can the true impact of systemic visibility be quantified.

[FRAMEWORK STEPS 6 & 9: EFFORT PER STEP, DELTA CALCULATION]

Instead of measuring report build time, the organization measured **time-to-know**.

Before vs After (Representative)

- Before: 3–5 days from period close to validated insight
- After: same-day visibility, often within hours

Effort per Cycle (Before)

- ~12 hours of analyst effort per weekly cycle:
  - Extraction
  - Reconciliation
  - Validation
  - Explanation

Effort per Cycle (After)

- ~4 hours per cycle:
  - Monitoring
  - Exception review
  - Interpretation

Effort Delta per Cycle

- 8 hours saved per weekly cycle

The reduction in time-to-know is the operational breakthrough of this chapter. It captures both speed and trust in a single measure.

Effort drops not because work disappears but because it changes shape. Assembly gives way to monitoring. Explanation gives way to interpretation.

This delta is durable. As volume increases, the gap widens in favor of the after state. Faster cycles do not require more analysts—they require better flow.

By measuring what matters, the organization ensures that improvement targets the decision itself, not just the mechanics around it.

Behavioral change driven by faster decisions

Behavior follows timing.

When information arrives late, organizations adapt by debating, buffering, and escalating. When information arrives early, they act. Faster visibility does not just change efficiency—it changes posture.[6]

Scaling the improvement across time reveals why this matters. What feels like a modest weekly gain compounds into meaningful capacity over a year.

Applying a blended rate grounds the analysis without overstating impact. The intent is not to claim secondary benefits but to establish a conservative baseline that can be trusted.[7]

This is where system design translates into economic language.

(FRAMEWORK STEPS 7 & 8: SCALE ACROSS TIME, APPLY BLENDED RATE)

Scaling the Improvement

- Weekly cycles per year: 52
- Hours avoided per cycle: 8
- Annual hours avoided: 8 × 52 = 416 hours

Blended Rate Assumption

Using the same logic as the value tracker (senior analysts, fully loaded cost):

- $150/hour blended rate

Annualized Value (Explicit Math)

416 hours × $150/hour = $62,400 per year

This calculation includes **only:**

- Reduced analyst preparation and reconciliation time

It explicitly **excludes:**

- Faster corrective actions
- Reduced downstream operational impact
- Improved commercial outcomes

Those benefits exist but are not claimed to remain conservative.

The calculated savings are intentionally narrow, yet they are persistent. Every cycle avoided reinforces the same behavioral shift: act sooner, adjust earlier, argue less.

The excluded benefits—faster corrections, reduced downstream impact, improved outcomes—are not speculative. They are simply harder to isolate cleanly. Their omission strengthens the credibility of the claim.

What remains is a reliable, recurring return driven by time reclaimed and attention redirected.

This is how faster decisions show up financially: not as dramatic spikes, but as steady structural advantage.

The collapsed decision-cycle pattern

Patterns endure when they explain more than one instance.

The collapsed decision-cycle pattern applies wherever organizations rely on periodic reconciliation to understand continuous reality. It is not specific to reporting tools, industries, or data domains.[8]

By shortening the distance between event and awareness, the organization reduces both effort and error—not once but every time the cycle repeats.[9]

This makes the pattern reusable. Anywhere decisions wait on validation, the same opportunity exists.

[FRAMEWORK STEP 10: TRANSLATE INTO BUSINESS LANGUAGE]

This example demonstrates a reusable pattern:

When organizations shorten the distance between reality and awareness, they reduce both effort and error—repeatedly.

BUSINESS TRANSLATION

This initiative delivered:

- **Recurring labor savings** through reduced reconciliation
- **Faster decisions** at every review cycle
- **Higher confidence** in operational and executive discussions

More importantly, it changed behavior:

- Decisions moved closer to events
- Fewer corrections were required later
- Trust replaced debate

This is not reporting efficiency.
It is decision effectiveness at scale.
What ultimately changes is not just speed but trust.

When reality and insight move closer together, debate gives way to dialogue. Decisions become about direction, not defense. Corrections are smaller because they happen earlier.

This is why the pattern scales. It improves outcomes without requiring heroics, discipline, or constant intervention.

The organization does not just decide faster. It decides better—consistently.

This is not reporting efficiency.

It is operational intelligence designed into the system.

Tying it all together

The concepts in this chapter focus on decision latency as a hidden operational cost.

To make that idea concrete, the following example shows how collapsing decision cycles can be translated into measurable business value.

Using a standard value articulation framework, it traces the path from delayed insight, through system-level visibility, to a quantified outcome.

The sections are shown exactly as they would appear in practice, illustrating how faster awareness is converted into defensible, business-relevant impact.

1. TITLE

Reducing Decision Latency Through System-Level Performance Visibility

2. CURRENT SITUATION

(In business terms, what was the gap or the need?)

Operational and commercial leaders relied on recurring performance views spanning sales, supply chain, and financial metrics to guide weekly and monthly decisions.

While the required data existed across systems, validated insight was only available after manual extraction, reconciliation, and review.

This created a recurring business gap:

- Decisions were routinely delayed until reporting cycles completed
- Corrections were applied after performance had already drifted
- Analysts spent significant time assembling and validating data rather than interpreting it
- Leaders increasingly relied on intuition when trusted data was not yet available

The issue was not lack of information. It was the time required to turn data into something decision-ready.

3. OBJECTIVE

(In business terms, what was the business trying to solve?)

The business objective was to shorten the time between operational reality and executive awareness without increasing reporting effort or analytical headcount.

Specifically, the organization aimed to:

- Provide timely, trusted performance visibility aligned to decision cadence
- Reduce analyst effort spent on manual reconciliation and report preparation
- Enable leaders to identify drift and intervene earlier in the cycle
- Create a repeatable model where faster decisions did not depend on heroic effort

4. SOLUTION

(What was the solution, and how did analytics products/services assist?)

A shared performance layer was implemented with standardized definitions embedded upstream and automated validation applied before metrics were consumed.

Key elements of the solution included:

- Consistent performance definitions enforced at the data layer
- Automated refresh and reconciliation routines aligned to operational cadence
- Direct access for decision-makers to validated performance views
- Analysts refocused on exception analysis and interpretation rather than assembly

Analytics products enabled visibility to function as a system capability rather than a manual reporting task.

5. BUSINESS VALUE

(Describe the business value in VERY SPECIFIC terms.)

This initiative materially reduced the time and effort required to reach decision-ready insight.

As a result:

- Weekly performance views became available the same day rather than days after close

- Analyst effort dedicated to reconciliation and preparation declined significantly
- Decision discussions shifted from debating numbers to acting on them
- Fewer late-cycle corrections were required due to earlier detection of drift

The core value was not faster reports—it was faster, more confident decisions made closer to real events.

6. BUSINESS VALUE CALCULATION DETAILS

(Describe in very specific terms HOW the business value was calculated.)

To quantify value, the organization measured analyst effort required per decision cycle before and after the change.

Assumptions (Conservative):

- Weekly operational review cycles: ~50 per year
- Analyst effort per cycle before automation: ~10 hours
- Analyst effort per cycle after automation: ~3 hours

Effort Delta per Cycle:

- 10 hours (before) – 3 hours (after) = 7 hours saved

Annual Effort Avoided:

- 7 hours × 50 cycles = 350 hours per year

Blended Fully Loaded Rate:

- Senior analysts and reporting roles: ~$160/hour

7. TOTAL AMOUNT OF VALUE FOR THE YEAR (IN $)

350 hours × $160/hour = ~$56,000 per year

$56,000 cost avoided Year 1
$168,000 cost avoided Year 3

This figure represents **direct labor efficiency from reduced preparation and reconciliation effort.**

It intentionally excludes:

- Financial impact of faster corrective actions
- Avoided downstream operational disruption
- Improved commercial outcomes from earlier intervention

CHAPTER 12

MAKING THE SUPPLY CHAIN SELF-AWARE

"If you don't like something, change it. If you can't change it, change your attitude."

— MAYA ANGELOU

Operating blind in a high-variance environment

Supply chains are not stable systems. Variance is not an exception—it is the operating condition. Demand shifts unexpectedly. Lead times compress or stretch. Partners behave unevenly. In this environment, awareness is not a convenience; it is a prerequisite for control.[1]

Yet many organizations attempt to manage variance with lagging signals. Inventory positions are reviewed after they are reported, validated after they are aggregated, and acted on after impact has already occurred. The result is not negligence but blindness—a structural inability to see conditions as they form.

When awareness lags reality, even well-designed processes become reactive. Teams respond to outcomes rather than trajectories. Risk is discovered through service failure or financial variance instead of early indicators.[2]

To understand how this happens, we must define the before state clearly. Not in terms of intent or effort but in terms of how current the organization's understanding actually is. Only then can we see how operating blind becomes normalized—and costly—in high-variance environments.

[FRAMEWORK STEP 1: DEFINE BEFORE STATE]

Supply chains operate under constant variance: demand shifts, lead times fluctuate, and partner behavior is uneven.

In this example, the organization relied on downstream distribution partners to hold and report inventory positions critical to planning, finance, and commercial execution.

Inventory data existed, but awareness lagged reality.

The organization faced recurring problems:

- Inventory positions were stale by the time they were reviewed
- Exceptions surfaced after service or financial impact
- Teams operated reactively instead of proactively

The supply chain was not unmanaged—it was under-informed.

The before state makes one constraint unmistakable: The organization did not lack data. It lacked timely awareness.

Inventory positions were known—just not when they mattered most. By the time issues surfaced, the cost of intervention had already increased. Decisions were reactive not because teams were inattentive but because insight arrived too late to be preventive.

This is the defining risk of lagging visibility in supply chains. Variance does not announce itself. It accumulates quietly until thresholds are crossed.

By naming this condition explicitly, the organization reframes the problem. The issue is not partner performance or analytical rigor. It is the structural delay between reality and recognition—a delay that compounds as scale and complexity increase.

Manual creation of operational awareness

In many supply chain environments, this assembly work is accepted as inevitable. Partners send files. Analysts reconcile formats. Metrics are recalculated. Exceptions are reviewed—all after conditions have already changed.

This model creates the illusion of control while masking its fragility. Awareness exists only at discrete moments, dependent on coordination across organizations and roles. Between cycles, the system is effectively blind.[3]

To expose the cost of this approach, we must map the process as it truly operates and identify who carries the burden. Frequency matters here. When manual assembly repeats every week, the effort and delay become structural.[4]

Operational awareness, in this state, is not continuous. It is recreated from scratch, one cycle at a time.

(FRAMEWORK STEPS 3–5: PROCESS STEPS, ACTORS, FREQUENCY)

Actors Identified

- Supply Chain Analysts
- Finance Analysts
- Commercial Operations
- External Distribution Partners

Before-State Process (Mapped)

1. Partners delivered inventory files on a scheduled basis
2. Analysts manually ingested and standardized the data
3. Days-on-hand and inventory health metrics recalculated
4. Exceptions reviewed after compilation
5. Follow-up initiated once issues were already present

Frequency Captured

- Inventory files received weekly
- Manual preparation and reconciliation required each cycle
- Issues often discovered days after conditions changed

Operational awareness was assembled manually, one cycle at a time.

This process reveals why reaction becomes the default mode. Exceptions are identified only after compilation. Follow-up begins only once issues are already present.

The manual mechanics are not inefficient because they are poorly executed. They are inefficient because they occur too late in the signal chain. Validation after aggregation guarantees delay. Review after compilation guarantees surprise.

By mapping steps, actors, and frequency, the organization makes visible what was previously diffuse: Awareness itself had become a recurring project.

And projects do not scale with variance. Systems do.

Automation as organizational sensing

Automation is often framed as a labor-saving tactic. In this case, that framing is incomplete.

What the organization sought was not faster reporting but earlier perception. The goal was to sense conditions as they emerged, not to summarize them after the fact.

Reframing inventory visibility as organizational sensing changes the design criteria. Timeliness becomes primary. Consistency becomes mandatory. Human effort shifts from construction to interpretation.[5]

This is a system-level change. It alters how information enters the enterprise, how it is validated, and how frequently it is refreshed. Most importantly, it collapses the distance between external reality and internal awareness.[6]

Defining the after state in these terms makes clear that automation is not the outcome. Awareness is.[7]

[FRAMEWORK STEP 2: DEFINE AFTER STATE]

The organization reframed inventory visibility as an organizational sensing capability, not a reporting exercise.

After State Defined (Anonymized)

- Automated ingestion of partner inventory feeds
- Standardized inventory and days-on-hand calculations
- Embedded validation rules at ingestion
- Consistent refresh cadence aligned to operational reality

Instead of static snapshots, inventory became a continuously refreshed signal.

Human effort shifted from data assembly to exception interpretation.

In the after state, inventory is no longer a static artifact. It is a living signal.

Because ingestion is automated and rules are enforced at entry, trust is established immediately. Because refresh aligns to operational cadence, awareness tracks reality rather than trailing it.

Human effort is not reduced by simplification alone. It is reduced because humans are no longer responsible for creating awareness—only for interpreting what the system already sees.

This is the difference between reporting on the supply chain and sensing it.

Reducing surprise through early visibility

In high-variance systems, surprise is expensive.

The later an issue is discovered, the fewer options remain and the higher the cost of intervention. Yet traditional metrics focus on effort saved rather than risk avoided.[8]

By measuring effort per cycle and calculating deltas, the organization quantifies what disappears when awareness becomes continuous. But the more important outcome lies beneath the math: the reduction of surprise itself.

Early visibility changes not just workload but timing. It shifts detection upstream, where corrective action is cheaper, faster, and less disruptive.

This is where operational sensing begins to pay dividends beyond labor efficiency.

[FRAMEWORK STEPS 6 & 9: EFFORT PER STEP, DELTA CALCULATION]

Effort per Cycle (Before)

- Manual ingestion, validation, reconciliation
- Exception identification performed after compilation

Effort per Cycle (After)

- Automated ingestion and calculation
- Human review focused only on true exceptions

Measured Delta (from Excel)

- 1,205 hours per year eliminated from manual inventory processing and analysis

This delta represents:

- Fewer manual ingestion steps
- Fewer reconciliation cycles
- Earlier detection of inventory risk

The most valuable reduction was not effort alone—it was surprise avoided.

The measured reduction in hours captures only part of the value. It reflects fewer manual steps, fewer reconciliations, and fewer late-stage investigations.

What it does not fully capture—by design—is the cost of issues that never escalated because they were seen forming.

Surprise avoided rarely shows up in financial statements. It shows up as stability, service continuity, and calmer operations.

By collapsing the gap between condition and awareness, the organization traded reaction for anticipation. That trade is where risk begins to fall.

Scaling awareness across partners and nodes

Scale exposes design flaws.

As the number of partners, nodes, and transactions increases, manual awareness mechanisms degrade rapidly. Each additional feed adds effort. Each new partner introduces latency. Complexity grows faster than capacity.

Systemic awareness behaves differently. Once ingestion, validation, and refresh are automated, scale amplifies value instead of cost.[9]

Applying scale assumptions and a blended rate translates this structural difference into economic terms. The math is explicit, conservative, and grounded in actual operating roles.[10]

This is where sensing becomes a financial capability, not just a technical one.

[FRAMEWORK STEPS 7 & 8: SCALE ACROSS TIME, APPLY BLENDED RATE]

Scale Assumptions (Explicit)

- Weekly inventory cycles
- Multiple distribution partners
- Full operating year

Blended Rate Assumption

From the value tracker, the implied blended rate across supply chain, finance, and commercial analysts is:

$$\$183{,}837 \div 1{,}205 \text{ hours} \approx \$152/\text{hour}$$

This reflects:

- Senior analytical roles
- Cross-functional involvement
- Fully loaded enterprise cost

Annualized Value

$$1{,}205 \text{ hours} \times \$152/\text{hour} \approx \$183{,}837 \text{ per year}$$

This calculation excludes:

- Working capital optimization
- Reduced service risk
- Avoided commercial disruption

Those benefits are real but intentionally not claimed to remain conservative.

The resulting value is recurring and proportional to complexity. More partners do not require more analysts. They generate more signal.

By excluding secondary benefits, the calculation remains intentionally narrow. Yet even within that constraint, the impact is material and durable.

This is how organizations grow without multiplying coordination costs. Awareness scales because it is embedded, not staffed.

The supply chain becomes more complex—and, paradoxically, easier to manage.

The self-aware supply chain pattern

Patterns endure because they explain cause and effect across contexts.

The self-aware supply chain pattern applies wherever organizations depend on lagging indicators to manage fast-moving systems. It is not limited to inventory, partners, or logistics.[11]

When awareness lags reality, surprise becomes routine. When awareness is continuous, intervention moves upstream, and cost collapses.

This pattern reframes visibility as an operating capability, not a reporting artifact.

[FRAMEWORK STEP 10: TRANSLATE INTO BUSINESS LANGUAGE]

This example demonstrates a reusable enterprise pattern:

When awareness lags reality, organizations pay for surprise.

When awareness is continuous, cost collapses upstream.

BUSINESS TRANSLATION

This initiative delivered:

- **Direct labor savings** through automation
- **Risk reduction** through earlier detection
- **Better capital decisions** driven by current-state inventory

More importantly, it created a structural capability:

- Awareness scaled without adding analysts
- Each additional partner increased value, not effort

A self-aware supply chain:

- Sees issues forming
- Acts while intervention is cheap
- Converts data into foresight

A self-aware supply chain does not predict the future. It recognizes the present early enough to act.

By sensing conditions as they emerge, the organization shifts from firefighting to steering. Issues are addressed while options are plentiful and consequences are small.

The value compounds because the capability persists. Each new partner, node, or signal strengthens awareness without increasing effort.

This is not automation for efficiency.

This is awareness by design—and foresight as a system property.

Tying it all together

The patterns in this chapter focus on awareness as a system capability, not a reporting exercise.

To show how that shift translates into measurable impact, the following example walks through a real-world application using a standard business value framework.

It connects the move from reactive inventory monitoring to automated intelligence with a quantified operational outcome.

The sections are presented exactly as they would appear in practice, illustrating how earlier awareness is converted into defensible, business-relevant value.

1. TITLE

Automating Distributor Inventory Visibility to Reduce Effort and Avoid Surprise

2. CURRENT SITUATION

(In business terms, what was the gap or the need?)

The organization depended on downstream distribution partners to provide inventory data critical to supply planning, financial forecasting, and commercial decision-making. While inventory data was available, it arrived in periodic files that required manual ingestion, standardization, and reconciliation before it could be used.

This created a persistent business gap:

- Inventory positions were reviewed days after conditions changed
- Exceptions were discovered only after service or financial impact occurred
- Analysts spent significant time preparing data rather than interpreting it
- Supply chain decisions were reactive rather than anticipatory

The challenge was not access to data but the lack of timely, reliable awareness across partners.

3. OBJECTIVE

(In business terms, what was the business trying to solve?)

The business objective was to improve inventory awareness across distribution partners without increasing analytical workload or operational overhead.

Specifically, the organization aimed to:

- Reduce manual effort required to process partner inventory data
- Detect inventory risks earlier in the operating cycle
- Provide consistent, trusted inventory metrics across functions
- Enable proactive intervention rather than post-impact correction

4. SOLUTION

(What was the solution, and how did analytics products/services assist?)

An automated inventory intelligence capability was implemented to ingest partner data feeds, apply standardized calculations, and surface actionable signals on a recurring cadence.

Key elements of the solution included:

- Automated ingestion and validation of distributor inventory files
- Standardized days-on-hand and inventory health calculations
- Embedded quality checks to flag anomalies at ingestion
- Centralized visibility for supply chain, finance, and commercial teams

Analytics products transformed inventory data from a periodic report into a continuously refreshed operational signal.

5. BUSINESS VALUE

(Describe the business value in VERY SPECIFIC terms.)

This initiative eliminated a large portion of the manual effort previously required to create inventory visibility.

As a result:

- Analysts no longer manually ingested and reconciled partner inventory files

- Inventory health metrics were available earlier and more consistently
- Exceptions were identified closer to the moment conditions changed
- Teams shifted from assembling data to evaluating risk and taking action

The most significant outcome was structural:

Awareness scaled across partners without scaling analyst effort.

6. BUSINESS VALUE CALCULATION DETAILS

(Describe in very specific terms HOW the business value was calculated.)

To quantify value, the organization measured analyst effort required to process and analyze partner inventory data before and after automation.

Assumptions (Conservative):

- Inventory processing and analysis cycles occurred weekly
- Manual effort before automation: ~25 hours per week
- Residual effort after automation (monitoring and exception review): ~2 hours per week

Annual Effort Avoided:

- (25–2) = 23 hours × 52 weeks = ~1,196 hours per year

Blended Fully Loaded Rate:

- Supply chain, finance, and commercial analysts: ~$145/hour

7. TOTAL AMOUNT OF VALUE FOR THE YEAR (IN $)

1,196 hours × $145/hour ≈ ~$173,000 per year

$173,000 in cost avoided in Year 1
$519,000 in cost avoided in Year 3

This figure reflects direct labor capacity created through automation of inventory intelligence.

It intentionally excludes:

- Working capital optimization benefits
- Avoided service disruptions
- Commercial risk reduction

Those benefits exist but were not monetized to keep the estimate conservative and defensible.

CHAPTER 13

WHEN INSIGHT DELIVERY BECOMES A FEATURE, NOT A PROJECT

"The most dangerous kind of waste is the waste we do not recognize."

— SHIGEO SHINGO

Why analytics projects fail to reach steady state

Most analytics initiatives do not fail outright. They fade.

They begin with urgency, funding, and attention. Early wins create optimism. Over time, however, delivery becomes uneven. Backlogs grow. Timelines slip. Stakeholders lose confidence—not because insight lacks value but because it cannot be produced reliably.[1]

This pattern is often misdiagnosed as a resourcing problem or a tooling gap. More analysts are hired. New platforms are introduced. Yet the underlying delivery model remains unchanged.

The core issue is not analytical capability. It is the absence of a steady-state operating model for insight delivery.

When every question is treated as a project, analytics behaves like bespoke craft work. That model does not scale with demand, no matter how talented the team.

To understand why analytics stalls, we must define the before state precisely—not by outputs delivered but by how work is structured, repeated, and absorbed over time.

[FRAMEWORK STEP 1: DEFINE BEFORE STATE]

Analytics initiatives often start strong and stall quietly.

In this example, the organization had no shortage of analytical talent or tooling. What it lacked was a **steady-state delivery model**. Each new question, enhancement, or metric adjustment was treated as a discrete project.

Common symptoms included:

- A growing backlog of "small" requests
- Highly skilled analysts spending time on repetitive logic
- Inconsistent results across similar analyses
- Delivery timelines that varied unpredictably

The issue was not demand.

It was that insight delivery did not scale.

The before state exposes a structural mismatch. Demand for insight was continuous and growing, while delivery was episodic and handcrafted.

Analysts were busy, but throughput was unpredictable. Similar questions produced different answers. Small changes required disproportionate effort. None of this reflected a lack of skill.

It reflected a delivery model optimized for novelty, not repetition.

When analytics lacks a steady state, every new request competes for attention, and every delivery feels urgent. Over time, this erodes trust—not in the data but in the system's ability to respond.

By naming this condition explicitly, the organization shifts the conversation. The problem is not execution. It is how insight itself is produced.

The cost of one-off insight delivery

One-off delivery feels responsive. Each request is handled carefully. Each artifact is tailored to the question at hand.

Yet beneath this responsiveness lies hidden cost.

When logic is rewritten repeatedly, definitions enforced late, and validation performed manually, effort accumulates without compounding benefit. Each delivery stands alone. Nothing gets easier the next time.[2]

This is the defining weakness of project-based analytics. Learning does not compound. Capacity does not expand. Familiar work still requires full effort.

To quantify this cost, we must examine the mechanics of delivery: who is involved, how work progresses, and how often similar requests recur. Frequency is what transforms customization from flexibility into constraint.[3]

[FRAMEWORK STEPS 3–5: PROCESS STEPS, ACTORS, FREQUENCY]

Actors Identified

- Analytics Engineers
- Business Analysts
- Data Platform Support
- Business Stakeholders

Before-State Process (Mapped)

1. Request submitted and clarified
2. Analyst locates relevant data assets
3. Logic written or modified manually
4. Results reviewed and validated
5. Output delivered as a custom artifact

Even familiar requests required rework because:

- Logic was duplicated across assets
- Definitions were enforced late
- Validation was repeated manually

Frequency Captured

- Enhancement requests arrived weekly
- Mix of net-new questions and variations on existing ones
- Backlog grew faster than delivery capacity

Insight delivery behaved like craft work, not production.

The mapped process reveals why backlogs grow despite constant effort. Each request triggers the same sequence of clarification, reconstruction, and validation—even when the question is only a variation on something already answered.

Because logic is duplicated, trust must be rebuilt each time. Because validation is manual, timelines stretch unpredictably.

Insight delivery behaves like artisanal production: high skill, low leverage.

This model cannot absorb increasing demand. It does not fail catastrophically. It degrades gradually—until responsiveness becomes the exception rather than the rule.

Embedding insight directly into platforms

A scalable analytics model does not eliminate complexity. It contains it.

By embedding insight into platforms, the organization shifts from bespoke construction to component assembly. Reuse becomes the default. Validation becomes systemic. Consistency becomes automatic.

This reframing changes the analyst's role. Instead of recreating logic, analysts design the patterns others rely on. Instead of validating outputs repeatedly, they validate the system that produces them.[4]

The goal is not speed alone. It is reliability.

Defining the after state at this level makes clear that analytics is no longer a service queue. It is an internal product—one that delivers insight continuously, predictably, and at scale.

[FRAMEWORK STEP 2: DEFINE AFTER STATE]

The organization reframed analytics as a platform capability, not a queue of projects.

After State Defined (Anonymized)

- Standardized semantic models for core domains
- Reusable analytical patterns for common calculations
- Assisted development workflows for repetitive logic
- Built-in validation and testing routines

Instead of rebuilding insight, analysts assembled it from trusted components.

Human effort shifted:

- From writing similar logic repeatedly
- To designing, validating, and extending reusable patterns

Insight became embedded, not delivered.

In the after state, insight is no longer delivered as a custom artifact. It is accessed as a feature.

Because semantic models and patterns are standardized, results are consistent across contexts. Because workflows are assisted, repetitive effort collapses. Because validation is built in, trust travels with the insight.

Human effort shifts upward—from execution to design.

This is the foundation of steady-state analytics: not faster projects, but fewer projects altogether.

AI as a throughput multiplier for analytics

Productivity gains in analytics are often framed in minutes saved per task. That framing understates the real leverage.

The constraint in analytics is rarely individual task duration. It is throughput—how many meaningful questions the organization can answer reliably over time.[5]

By introducing pattern-based and assisted development, the organization changes how effort translates into output.

Analysts spend less time on mechanics and more time on extension.

The result is not marginal efficiency. It is multiplicative capacity.

This is where AI creates value—not by replacing analysts but by amplifying their ability to produce consistent, validated insight.[6]

(FRAMEWORK STEPS 6 & 9: EFFORT PER STEP, DELTA CALCULATION)

The primary delta in this example is **throughput**, not time saved per task.

Before-State Throughput

- Average analyst capacity: **3–4 meaningful enhancements per week**
- Significant time spent on repetitive transformations and validation

After-State Throughput

- Pattern-based and assisted development reduced manual steps
- Average analyst capacity increased to **6–8 enhancements per week**

Net Throughput Delta (Conservative)

- Incremental capacity: **+3 enhancements per analyst per week**

This improvement did not require:

- More headcount
- Longer hours
- Reduced quality

It came from leverage.

The throughput delta is the critical metric here. It captures leverage without overstating savings.

No hours were eliminated. No quality was sacrificed. No heroics were required.

Capacity increased because friction decreased.

This is the hallmark of a well-designed system: more output from the same inputs achieved through structure rather than pressure.

AI functions here as a force multiplier—applied where repetition previously consumed expertise.

Moving from delivery speed to delivery reliability

Organizations often chase faster delivery without addressing why timelines vary in the first place. Reliability, by contrast, emerges when delivery is no longer reinvented for each request.[7]

By translating throughput gains into FTE-equivalent value, the organization quantifies capacity creation without claiming cost elimination. This distinction matters. It preserves credibility.

The value here is not budget reduction. It is avoided constraint—the ability to meet demand growth without proportional headcount growth.[8]

This is how analytical leverage shows up economically.

TRANSLATING CAPACITY INTO VALUE (EXPLICIT ASSUMPTION)

Rather than pricing each enhancement, the organization translated capacity into FTE-equivalent value.

- Fully loaded cost of analytics engineer: $160,000/year

If assisted development creates ~30–35% capacity uplift, then:

$\$160{,}000 \times 30\% \approx \$48{,}000$ per year

This represents avoided hiring or deferred headcount growth, not cash removed from the budget.

WHY THIS IS CONSERVATIVE

This calculation:

- Excludes business value of faster insights
- Excludes avoided rework downstream
- Excludes improved consistency and trust

It prices capacity only.

The conservative valuation reinforces the point. Even when pricing capacity alone, the benefit is material and recurring.

Excluded benefits—faster decisions, reduced rework, increased trust—are real but not required to justify the investment.

By shifting from delivery speed to delivery reliability, analytics becomes predictable. Backlogs stabilize. Stakeholder confidence returns.

Capacity becomes structural, not heroic.

The insight-as-a-feature pattern

Patterns matter because they travel.

The insight-as-a-feature pattern applies wherever analytics demand grows faster than delivery capacity. It reframes insight from a service outcome into a platform capability.[9]

When insight is embedded, marginal delivery cost approaches zero. Each new question builds on what already exists.[10]

This is how analytics escapes the project trap.

[FRAMEWORK STEP 10: TRANSLATE INTO BUSINESS LANGUAGE]

This example demonstrates a powerful pattern:

When insight is treated as a feature of the platform, marginal delivery cost collapses.

BUSINESS TRANSLATION

This initiative delivered:

- **More insight with the same team**
- **Predictable delivery**, not heroic effort
- **Consistent results** across the organization

The value is not "AI productivity." The value is reliable analytical throughput.

When insight becomes a feature:

- Backlogs stop growing
- Quality stabilizes
- Scale becomes structural

When insight becomes a feature, organizations stop paying for the same understanding repeatedly.

Delivery stabilizes. Quality becomes consistent. Scale stops being painful.

This is not an AI story. It is a systems story.

AI enables leverage, but the value comes from design—from treating analytics as infrastructure rather than output.

Together with prior chapters, this completes the arc:

- Flow (Chapter 10)
- Decision latency (Chapter 11)
- Awareness (Chapter 12)
- Capacity (Chapter 13)

Same framework.

Different constraint.

Same result: structural value that compounds.

Tying it all together

This chapter reframes analytics value from speed of delivery to reliability of capacity.

To ground that shift in measurable terms, the following example shows how treating insight as a platform feature translates into quantifiable business impact.

Using a standard value articulation framework, it connects reusable analytical patterns and assisted development to increased delivery throughput.

The sections below are presented as they would be in practice, illustrating how analytical leverage becomes defensible, business-relevant value.

1. TITLE

Increasing Analytical Throughput Without Increasing Headcount

2. CURRENT SITUATION

(In business terms, what was the gap or the need?)

The organization relied on analytics to support operational and commercial decisions but insight delivery was treated as a series of discrete projects. Each new question or enhancement required analysts to locate data, recreate logic, validate results, and deliver a custom output.

This created a recurring business gap:

- A growing backlog of enhancement requests
- Highly skilled analysts spending time on repetitive transformations
- Inconsistent results across similar analyses
- Delivery timelines that varied unpredictably

The constraint was not demand or talent. It was that insight delivery did not scale with volume.

3. OBJECTIVE

(In business terms, what was the business trying to solve?)

The business objective was to increase the organization's capacity to deliver analytical insights without adding analytical headcount or extending delivery timelines.

Specifically, the organization aimed to:

- Reduce repeated effort across similar analytical requests
- Improve consistency and reliability of results
- Increase the number of enhancements delivered per analyst
- Shift analytics work from bespoke development to structured assembly

4. SOLUTION

(What was the solution, and how did analytics products/ services assist?)

Analytics delivery was restructured around reusable assets and assisted development workflows.

Key elements of the solution included:

- Standardized semantic models for core business domains
- Reusable calculation and transformation patterns
- Embedded validation and testing routines
- Assisted development features that reduced manual coding for common logic

Analytics products enabled insight to be assembled from trusted components, rather than rebuilt for each request.

5. BUSINESS VALUE

(Describe the business value in VERY SPECIFIC terms.)

This initiative increased the volume of analytical enhancements that could be delivered by the same team.

As a result:

- Analysts completed more enhancements per week without working longer hours
- Backlogs stabilized instead of growing
- Results became more consistent across similar use cases
- Delivery became predictable rather than dependent on individual effort

The primary value was not time saved on a task—it was capacity created across the system.

6. BUSINESS VALUE CALCULATION DETAILS

(Describe in very specific terms HOW the business value was calculated.)

To quantify value, the organization measured changes in analyst throughput before and after implementing reusable analytics patterns.

Assumptions (Conservative):

- Average analyst throughput before: ~3 enhancements per week
- Average analyst throughput after: ~6 enhancements per week
- Incremental capacity: +3 enhancements per week
- Working weeks per year: ~48

Annual Incremental Capacity:

- 3 enhancements × 48 weeks = 144 additional enhancements per year

Rather than pricing individual enhancements, the organization translated capacity into FTE-equivalent value.

Fully Loaded Analyst Cost:

- ~$155,000 per year

Conservative Capacity Uplift Assumption:

- ~30% effective capacity gain

7. TOTAL AMOUNT OF VALUE FOR THE YEAR (IN $)

$155,000 × 30% ≈ ~$46,500 per year

$46,500 cost avoided in Year 1
$139,500 cost avoided in Year 3

This figure reflects avoided hiring or deferred headcount growth through increased analytical throughput.

It intentionally excludes:

- Business value of faster decisions
- Reduced rework from consistent definitions
- Improved trust and adoption

Those benefits exist but were not monetized to keep the estimate conservative and credible.

CHAPTER 14

MOVING THE PAST WITHOUT FREEZING THE FUTURE

"It is not the strongest of the species that survives, nor the most intelligent, but the one most responsive to change."

— CHARLES DARWIN

Why migrations stall organizational progress

Data migrations are often framed as technical events: Move data from here to there, validate it, and proceed. In reality, migrations are organizational choke points. They determine whether modernization accelerates progress or freezes it.

Most migrations do not fail loudly. They linger. Timelines stretch. Dependencies pile up. Teams wait. What was intended to enable transformation becomes the reason transformation slows.[1]

This happens because migration forces the organization to confront its own history—accumulated decisions, undocumented logic, and structures optimized for a past reality. Every inconsistency must be interpreted before progress can continue.[2]

When modernization depends on fully translating the past, forward momentum becomes hostage to historical complexity.

To understand why migrations stall progress, we must define the before state not as a technical shortcoming but as a structural condition: progress paced by translation. Only then can we see why organizations feel stuck even while large teams are actively working.

(FRAMEWORK STEP 1: DEFINE BEFORE STATE)

Data migrations rarely fail outright.

They stall.

In this example, the organization was modernizing a core platform while carrying years of accumulated historical structures:

- Legacy schemas
- Inconsistent naming conventions
- Undocumented relationships
- Embedded business logic only understood by a few individuals

Every modernization initiative depended on first translating the past into a new form.

As a result, forward progress slowed to the pace of migration.

The cost wasn't just delay.

It was organizational paralysis while waiting for history to move.

The before state reveals a subtle but powerful dynamic: the organization was not blocked by lack of effort, funding, or intent. It was blocked by dependency.

Every future-state initiative waited for the past to be fully understood, documented, and recreated. This created a form of organizational paralysis—not inactivity but motion without advancement.

Migration became the critical path for everything else. Innovation queued behind translation.

This is why migration stalls progress. It does not stop work. It stops flow.

By naming this condition explicitly, the organization reframes the challenge. The problem is not data quality or documentation discipline. It is allowing history to dictate the pace of the future.

Hidden effort and risk in translation and validation

Migration effort is often underestimated because much of it is invisible.

Manual analysis, iterative validation, and repeated correction cycles rarely appear as distinct line items. They are absorbed into project timelines and accepted as necessary friction.

Yet this friction carries both cost and risk. Each manual mapping introduces interpretation. Each validation cycle introduces delay. Each correction extends exposure to legacy systems.

To surface this hidden burden, we must map the process as it actually runs—across roles, phases, and repetitions. Frequency matters here. When translation work repeats across domains and systems, it becomes structural rather than incidental.

What looks like careful diligence at the task level becomes cumulative drag at the program level.

(FRAMEWORK STEPS 3–5: PROCESS STEPS, ACTORS, FREQUENCY)

Actors Identified

- Data Architects
- Migration Analysts
- Platform Engineers
- QA / Validation Specialists

Before-State Process (Mapped)

1. Legacy structures manually analyzed and documented
2. Target models designed in parallel but validated late
3. Field-by-field mappings created manually
4. Validation cycles executed iteratively
5. Corrections applied and revalidated

This process repeated across:

- Subject areas
- Source systems
- Migration phases

Frequency Captured

- Migration work executed in multi-week or multi-month phases
- Validation cycles repeated per domain
- Downstream teams blocked until completion

Migration became a **serial dependency**, not a parallel activity.

This process map shows why migration becomes serial by default. Translation and validation must complete before anything downstream can proceed.

Because the work is manual and iterative, timelines are uncertain. Because timelines are uncertain, dependencies wait. Because dependencies wait, coordination risk increases.

Migration stops being one activity among many. It becomes the gatekeeper for progress.

By identifying actors and frequency, the organization makes the cost of translation explicit. What was previously accepted as unavoidable effort is revealed as a design choice—one that can be challenged.

Decoupling historical data from forward progress

The breakthrough in this example was not better documentation. It was decoupling.

By reframing migration as a structural translation problem, the organization shifted its objective. The goal was no longer to perfectly reconstruct the past but to generate forward-compatible structures that could support progress immediately.

This required standardization, assisted extraction, and reusable mapping logic—not to eliminate human involvement but to reposition it.

Humans moved from redrawing history to validating outputs at scale.[3]

Decoupling history from progress changes the shape of modernization. Migration no longer blocks parallel work. Teams can move forward while translation continues in the background.[4]

This is not a shortcut. It is a change in dependency structure.

(FRAMEWORK STEP 2: DEFINE AFTER STATE)

The organization reframed migration as a **structural translation problem**, not a documentation exercise.

After State Defined (Anonymized)

- Standardized modeling patterns for common entities
- Assisted extraction of source structures
- Generated forward-compatible target models
- Reusable mapping logic applied consistently

Instead of serial translation, migration became parallelizable.

Human Role Shift

- From hand building and redrawing structures
- To validating, refining, and approving generated outputs

History still moved—but it no longer dictated the pace of progress.

In the after state, history still mattered—but it no longer governed pace.

By parallelizing translation and downstream work, the organization broke the serial dependency that had slowed everything else. Migration became an enabling stream rather than a bottleneck.

Human effort was elevated. Validation replaced reconstruction. Judgment replaced transcription.

This is the essence of forward compatibility: designing the future so it does not have to wait for the past to be perfectly understood.

Time compression as a form of risk reduction

Time is often treated as a delivery metric. In migrations, it is also a risk surface.[5]

Long-running migration phases extend exposure to legacy systems, increase coordination complexity, and multiply the chance of interruption. Dual-run environments persist. Teams context-switch. Assumptions age.[6]

Compressing time does more than accelerate delivery. It reduces uncertainty.

By focusing on time deltas rather than task elimination, the organization captures the true benefit of structural change: shorter windows of vulnerability.

This is where speed becomes safety.

(FRAMEWORK STEPS 6 & 9: EFFORT PER STEP, DELTA CALCULATION)

The most important delta in this example is **time**, not task elimination.

Before vs After (Representative)

- Before: migration phases lasting **16–20 weeks**
- After: equivalent scope completed in **8–10 weeks**

Effort Shift

- Fewer manual mapping and documentation steps
- Reduced validation rework
- Earlier engagement by downstream teams

Time Delta (Conservative)

- **~8 weeks per major migration phase** compressed

This compression reduced:

- Duration of dual-run environments
- Exposure to legacy system failure
- Program coordination risk

Time saved here is **risk avoided,** not just speed.

The compressed timeline reduced more than duration. It reduced the number of things that could go wrong.

Fewer weeks meant fewer handoffs, fewer changes in assumptions, and fewer opportunities for misalignment. Downstream teams engaged earlier, reducing rework and surprise.

Time saved here is not just efficiency gained. It is exposure avoided.

This is why time compression in migrations should be understood as risk reduction first—and speed second.

Quantifying the cost of standing still

Migration delays are often framed as opportunity costs—abstract and difficult to quantify. In reality, standing still has a very real economic footprint.[7]

Even when progress stalls, effort continues. Teams remain staffed. Legacy platforms stay online. Coordination overhead persists. Benefits wait.

By translating delay into weekly cost, the organization grounds the impact in operational reality. This is not hypothetical value. It is ongoing expenditure with deferred return.

Explicit assumptions matter here. They keep the calculation credible and conservative. The goal is not to inflate impact but to make inertia visible.[8]

This is where time becomes money—directly.

[FRAMEWORK STEPS 7 & 8: SCALE ACROSS TIME, APPLY BLENDED RATE]

Migration delay has an economic cost—even when no one is "doing nothing."

Standing-Still Cost Components

- Migration team effort continues
- Legacy platforms remain live
- Downstream teams wait or rework
- Benefits of the new platform are deferred

Explicit Assumptions

- Migration team size: 5 FTE
- Fully loaded blended rate: $150/hour
- Weekly effort per FTE: 40 hours

Cost per Week of Delay

5 FTE × 40 hours × $150/hour = $30,000 per week

Value of Time Compression

- Weeks avoided per phase: 8

8 weeks × $30,000/week = $240,000

This represents **cost avoided and value accelerated,** not hypothetical benefit.

It excludes:

- Earlier realization of future-state capabilities
- Reduced operational risk from legacy systems
- Improved morale and delivery predictability

Those benefits are real but not claimed here.

The resulting figure captures cost avoided and value accelerated, not imagined benefit.

Every week compressed removes real expense and unlocks downstream progress sooner. The excluded benefits—improved morale, reduced risk, earlier capability—would only strengthen the case.

By pricing delay explicitly, the organization reframes migration from a sunk-cost exercise to an economic lever.

Standing still is not neutral. It is expensive.

The forward-compatible migration pattern

Patterns endure when they change economics, not just timelines.

The forward-compatible migration pattern applies wherever historical complexity threatens to slow modernization. It replaces serial dependency with parallel progress.[9]

By allowing history to move without blocking the future, organizations stop paying interest on past decisions.

Migration becomes sustainable rather than episodic—something that supports evolution instead of interrupting it.[10]

(FRAMEWORK STEP 10: TRANSLATE INTO BUSINESS LANGUAGE)

This example demonstrates a reusable pattern:

When migration is allowed to block progress, the organization pays interest on the past.

BUSINESS TRANSLATION

This initiative delivered:

- **Material cost avoidance** through time compression
- **Reduced program risk** by shortening exposure windows
- **Earlier time-to-value** for modernization investments

More importantly, it changed the economics of migration:

- Progress no longer waited on perfect translation

- Teams moved forward while history caught up
- Modernization became sustainable instead of episodic

This is not faster migration.

It is forward-compatible delivery.

This pattern changes what migration means.

It is no longer a prerequisite to progress. It is a concurrent activity that improves over time. Teams move forward while translation catches up.

The value compounds because the capability persists. Each migration benefits from the same structure, the same patterns, the same decoupling.

This is not faster migration.

It is modernization without paralysis.

And with that, the framework comes full circle:

- Flow (Chapter 10)
- Decision (Chapter 11)
- Awareness (Chapter 12)
- Capacity (Chapter 13)
- Progress (Chapter 14)

Same framework.

Different constraint.

Structural value that endures.

Tying it all together

This chapter focuses on a form of value that is often overlooked: the cost of standing still.

To make that cost explicit, the following example shows how compressing migration timelines translates directly into measurable business value.

Using a standard value articulation framework, it connects time saved during modernization efforts to avoided cost and reduced exposure.

The sections are presented exactly as they would be in practice, illustrating how faster progress becomes defensible, business-relevant impact.

1. TITLE

Reducing Modernization Cost and Risk by Compressing Migration Timelines

2. CURRENT SITUATION

(In business terms, what was the gap or the need?)

The organization was modernizing core data platforms while carrying significant legacy structures, undocumented logic, and historical dependencies. Each modernization effort required extensive upfront translation of the past before forward progress could begin.

This created a recurring business gap:

- Migration phases stretched across multiple months
- Downstream teams were blocked waiting for historical data alignment
- Dual-run environments remained active longer than planned
- Program risk increased as timelines extended

The issue was not technical feasibility. It was that historical translation dictated the pace of progress.

3. OBJECTIVE

(In business terms, what was the business trying to solve?)

The business objective was to reduce the time and risk associated with data migration while allowing modernization initiatives to move forward in parallel.

Specifically, the organization aimed to:

- Shorten migration phases without increasing error rates
- Reduce the duration of parallel legacy and modern environments

- Lower the operational and coordination risk of extended programs
- Enable teams to realize modernization benefits sooner

4. SOLUTION

(What was the solution, and how did analytics products/services assist?)

Migration was reframed as a structural translation problem rather than a manual documentation exercise.

Key elements of the solution included:

- Standardized modeling patterns for common entities
- Assisted extraction and mapping of legacy structures
- Generated forward-compatible target models
- Reusable validation logic applied consistently across domains

Analytics products reduced manual mapping effort and enabled historical data to move in parallel with forward delivery.

5. BUSINESS VALUE

(Describe the business value in VERY SPECIFIC terms.)

This initiative materially reduced the duration of major migration phases.

As a result:

- Migration timelines were compressed by multiple weeks per phase
- Legacy environments were retired sooner, reducing operating exposure
- Downstream teams engaged earlier with modern platforms
- Program coordination risk declined as timelines shortened

The primary value was not faster delivery alone. It was **less time paying for delay and uncertainty.**

6. BUSINESS VALUE CALCULATION DETAILS

(Describe in very specific terms HOW the business value was calculated.)

To quantify value, the organization calculated the cost of extended migration timelines and the impact of compressing them.

Assumptions (Conservative):

- Average migration phase before improvement: ~18 weeks
- Average migration phase after improvement: ~10 weeks
- Time compressed per phase: ~8 weeks

Standing-Still Cost Assumptions:

- Migration team size: ~4 FTE
- Fully loaded blended rate: ~$155/hour
- Weekly effort per FTE: 40 hours

Cost per Week of Delay:

- 4 FTE × 40 hours × $155/hour ≈ $24,800 per week

Value of Time Compression:

- 8 weeks × $24,800/week ≈ $198,400

7. TOTAL AMOUNT OF VALUE FOR THE YEAR (IN $)

≈ $198,000 per major migration phase

$198,000 cost avoided in Year 1
$594,000 cost avoided in Year 3

This figure reflects **cost avoided and value accelerated through reduced migration duration.**

It intentionally excludes:

- Earlier realization of downstream business benefits
- Reduced incident risk from legacy systems
- Improved delivery predictability and morale

Those benefits exist but were not monetized to keep the estimate conservative and credible.

CHAPTER 15

PAYING ONLY FOR WHAT CREATES BUSINESS VALUE

"Rules are not necessarily sacred; principles are."

— FRANKLIN D. ROOSEVELT

Why cloud waste remains invisible

Cloud waste persists not because organizations are careless but because waste rarely looks like failure.

Systems stay online. Performance remains acceptable. Users do not complain. From an operational standpoint, everything appears healthy. From a financial standpoint, however, misalignment quietly accumulates.[1]

Cloud consumption is especially prone to this invisibility because provisioning decisions are often made early—during initial deployment—and then carried forward indefinitely. What was once prudent for uncertainty becomes excessive once usage stabilizes.[2]

Because nothing breaks, optimization feels risky. Teams fear touching stable systems. Finance sees rising spend but lacks the context to intervene safely. As a result, excess cost becomes normalized as the price of reliability.

To understand why cloud waste persists, we must define the before state not as mismanagement but as structural invisibility. The waste exists—but the system provides no signal that action is both necessary and safe.

[FRAMEWORK STEP 1: DEFINE BEFORE STATE]

Cloud waste rarely appears as a line item labeled "waste."

Instead, it hides inside:

- Overprovisioned service tiers
- Legacy configurations carried forward by default
- Resources sized for peak that operate at average load

In this example, multiple application environments were running on cloud service plans that were:

- Technically functional
- Operationally stable
- Economically misaligned with actual usage

No outages occurred.

No alarms fired.

And because nothing broke, nothing changed.

The before state reveals why cloud waste is so durable. It hides behind stability.

Because environments were technically sound and operationally quiet, there was no forcing function to revisit assumptions. Spend increased gradually, embedded in baseline run rates rather than flagged as anomalies.

This is the most dangerous form of inefficiency: cost without pain.

By naming this condition explicitly, the organization reframes the challenge. The problem is not overspending driven by negligence. It is misalignment sustained by silence.

Cloud waste remains invisible until the system is designed to reveal it.

Activity-based spend versus value-based consumption

Most cloud environments operate on an activity-based model by default. Resources are provisioned to support an application, and that configuration becomes the assumed cost of doing business.

What is rarely examined is whether that configuration continues to reflect actual value delivered.

When spend is reviewed in aggregate, inefficiency blends into the background. When optimization requires perceived risk, it is deferred. Over time, activity-based provisioning hardens into entitlement.[3]

To expose this misalignment, we must map not just the provisioning process, but the review cadence and decision rights around spend. Frequency matters here. Daily spend combined with quarterly review guarantees drift.[4]

Without workload-level visibility, cost remains something that happens—not something that is managed.

(FRAMEWORK STEPS 3–5: PROCESS STEPS, ACTORS, FREQUENCY)

Actors Identified

- Application Owners
- Platform Engineering
- Cloud Operations / FinOps
- Finance (chargeback / showback)

Before-State Process (Mapped)

1. Cloud resources provisioned during initial deployment
2. Configurations carried forward release after release
3. Spend reviewed in aggregate, not at workload level
4. Optimization deferred due to perceived risk

Frequency Captured

- Spend incurred **daily**
- Review cycles **quarterly at best**
- Rightsizing actions rare and reactive

Cloud consumption was activity-based: "This is what we provisioned."

It was not value-based: "This is what the business actually needs."

This before-state process explains why optimization was rare. No one owned the decision end-to-end.

Application teams owned functionality, not spend. Finance saw cost, not configuration. Platform teams avoided change to preserve stability.

As a result, consumption reflected historical activity rather than current need.

By making this distinction explicit—activity-based versus value-based—the organization identifies the missing link. Optimization was not avoided because it lacked benefit. It was avoided because it lacked a safe operating model.

Rightsizing without capability loss

Cloud optimization often fails because it is framed as reduction.

Reduction implies loss—of capacity, performance, or resilience. Even when savings are clear, teams resist actions that feel like downgrades.

Reframing optimization as alignment changes the conversation. The goal is not to remove capability, but to match resources to actual demand.[5]

This requires precise visibility, clear thresholds, and explicit validation. Optimization must be provably safe, not just economically attractive.

By defining the after state in these terms, the organization creates a path where optimization is no longer synonymous with risk. It becomes a controlled adjustment grounded in evidence.[6]

[FRAMEWORK STEP 2: DEFINE AFTER STATE]

The organization reframed optimization as **alignment**, not reduction.

After State Defined (Anonymized)

- Workload-level cost and utilization visibility
- Identification of overprovisioned service plans
- Generation upgrades and tier realignment
- Validation against performance and reliability thresholds

Crucially:

- No functionality was removed
- No availability targets were reduced
- No user-facing degradation occurred

Spend was aligned to **actual demand**, not historical assumptions.

The after state demonstrates a critical principle: Savings achieved without degradation are the most credible savings.

By validating performance and reliability explicitly, the organization removes fear from the optimization process. Teams no longer choose between cost and stability.

Spend is no longer a byproduct of history. It becomes a reflection of present demand.

This is how rightsizing becomes repeatable—not a one-time initiative but a safe operational practice.

Spend avoidance as the most credible savings

Savings claims often fail because they rely on aspiration rather than evidence.

Spend avoidance is different. It reflects a lower run rate that persists month after month. No assumptions about future behavior are required.[7]

By grounding optimization in specific, observable configuration changes—and measuring the resulting run-rate difference—the organization ensures credibility with both technical and financial stakeholders.[8]

This is not about clawing back past spend. It is about preventing unnecessary spend from recurring.

That distinction is what makes the savings real.

[FRAMEWORK STEPS 6 & 9: EFFORT PER STEP, DELTA CALCULATION]

This initiative focused on **spend avoidance**, not aspirational savings.

Representative Optimization Actions (from Tracker)

- App service plans running on higher-cost generations than required
- Production and non-production environments oversized relative to load

Measured Delta (from Excel Examples)

Two representative workloads delivered:

- **$285,600 annualized spend avoided**
- **$142,800 annualized spend avoided**

These savings came from:

- Lower unit cost per compute hour
- No increase in usage
- No change in application behavior

Importantly:

This was not a one-time rebate.

This was a **new, lower run rate.**

The measured deltas represent durable change. Nothing temporary. Nothing speculative.

Lower unit cost. Same usage. Same behavior.

Because these savings reset the baseline, they compound automatically. Each month that follows inherits the benefit.

This is the strongest form of financial impact: structural, verifiable, and repeatable.

Continuous optimization and compounding returns

Cloud economics reward early correction.

Because spend recurs, even modest misalignment multiplies over time. Conversely, once alignment is achieved, every future cycle benefits without additional effort.[9]

This is why optimization should not be treated as an event. It is a condition—a corrected run rate that persists.

By scaling the impact across time and environments, the organization shows how alignment compounds. Optimized patterns propagate. Mistakes are not repeated.[10]

The math here is intentionally conservative. It counts only what has already been realized, not what might be achieved later.

(FRAMEWORK STEPS 7 & 8: SCALE ACROSS TIME, APPLY RATE)

Cloud optimization compounds because spend recurs.

Annualized Impact (Explicit)

- For a single optimized workload:
- Monthly spend avoided × 12 = Annual value

Once aligned:

- Every future month benefits
- Every environment copied from the optimized pattern inherits savings
- Every new deployment avoids repeating the mistake

Why This Is Conservative

These calculations:

- Exclude future workload growth
- Exclude secondary optimizations
- Exclude improved forecasting accuracy

They count **only what is already proven.**

Optimization here is not an event.

It is a **run-rate correction.**

Once alignment is established, optimization becomes self-reinforcing.

New deployments inherit the corrected pattern. Future growth occurs on a lower cost curve. Forecasting improves because spend behavior stabilizes.

The organization does not need to hunt for savings repeatedly. The system prevents waste from re-emerging.

This is how cloud optimization becomes an operating advantage rather than a recurring firefight.

The value-aligned spend pattern

Patterns endure when they change incentives and behavior.

The value-aligned spend pattern reframes cloud cost from something to be cut into something to be managed intelligently. It aligns technical decisions with economic outcomes.[11]

When consumption reflects value delivered, optimization ceases to be adversarial. It becomes part of normal operations.[12]

This pattern applies anywhere usage-based pricing meets static assumptions.

[FRAMEWORK STEP 10: TRANSLATE INTO BUSINESS LANGUAGE]

This example demonstrates a powerful enterprise pattern:

When consumption is aligned to value, cost reduction becomes structural instead of episodic.

BUSINESS TRANSLATION

This initiative delivered:

- **Hard-dollar, finance-verifiable savings**
- **No loss of capability or performance**
- **Recurring value that compounds over time**

It also changed behavior:

- Optimization became safe
- Rightsizing became routine
- Spend conversations moved from "cut" to "align"

This is not cloud cost cutting.

It is **value-aligned consumption.**

Value-aligned consumption changes the economics of the cloud.

Savings are not episodic. They are structural. Teams do not fear optimization. They expect it.

By grounding decisions in evidence and preserving capability, the organization makes alignment sustainable.

This is not cloud cost cutting.

It is cloud economics done correctly.

And, with this chapter, the framework completes its final turn:

- Flow (Chapter 10)
- Decision latency (Chapter 11)
- Awareness (Chapter 12)
- Capacity (Chapter 13)
- Progress (Chapter 14)
- Economics (Chapter 15)

Same framework.

Different lever.

Enduring value.

Tying it all together

This chapter challenges the assumption that cloud cost reduction requires cutting capability.

To make that distinction concrete, the following example shows how aligning consumption to actual business demand produces measurable, recurring value.

Using a standard business value framework, it connects workload-level visibility and rightsizing to a defensible financial outcome.

The sections are presented exactly as they would be in practice, illustrating how spend alignment becomes a durable business result rather than a one-time savings exercise.

1. TITLE

Reducing Recurring Cloud Spend Through Value-Aligned Rightsizing

2. CURRENT SITUATION

(In business terms, what was the gap or the need?)

Multiple business-critical applications were running on cloud service configurations that had been provisioned conservatively and carried forward unchanged over time.

While performance and availability targets were being met, resource consumption no longer reflected actual usage patterns.

This created a persistent business gap:

- Cloud spend grew steadily without corresponding increases in business output
- Overprovisioned environments operated below capacity most of the time
- Optimization was deferred due to perceived risk of service degradation
- Cost discussions focused on totals, not on value delivered by individual workloads

The issue was not waste caused by failure. It was misalignment between consumption and need.

3. OBJECTIVE

(In business terms, what was the business trying to solve?)

The business objective was to reduce recurring cloud run rate without impacting application performance, reliability, or user experience.

Specifically, the organization aimed to:

- Align cloud resource consumption to actual workload demand
- Avoid unnecessary spend baked into baseline configurations

- Create a repeatable optimization approach that could scale safely
- Deliver finance-verifiable savings without operational tradeoffs

4. SOLUTION

(What was the solution, and how did analytics products/services assist?)

Workload-level cost and utilization analytics were used to identify misalignment between provisioned capacity and observed demand.

Key elements of the solution included:

- Detailed visibility into usage patterns by environment and workload
- Identification of service plans operating above required tiers
- Generation upgrades and tier realignment based on empirical data
- Validation of performance and stability post-change

Analytics products enabled optimization decisions to be evidence-based rather than assumption-driven.

5. BUSINESS VALUE

(Describe the business value in VERY SPECIFIC terms.)

This initiative permanently lowered the cost to run targeted applications.

As a result:

- Monthly cloud spend was reduced without changing application behavior
- Performance and availability remained within established thresholds
- Savings recurred automatically each billing cycle
- Optimized configurations became the new standard for future deployments

The value was structural: a lower run-rate, not a one-time reduction.

6. BUSINESS VALUE CALCULATION DETAILS

(Describe in very specific terms HOW the business value was calculated.)

To quantify value, the organization compared pre- and post-optimization cloud run rates for selected workloads.

Representative Adjustments (Conservative):

- Workload A: ~$23,000 per month in avoided spend
- Workload B: ~$12,000 per month in avoided spend

Annualized Value Calculation:

- ($23,000 + $12,000) × 12 months
- ≈ $420,000 per year in recurring spend avoidance

These figures reflect confirmed billing reductions following optimization and exclude projected or speculative savings.

7. TOTAL AMOUNT OF VALUE FOR THE YEAR (IN $)

≈ $420,000 per year

$420,000 cost avoided in Year 1
$1,260,000 cost avoided in Year 3

This figure represents hard-dollar, finance-verifiable recurring savings from value-aligned cloud consumption. It intentionally excludes:

- Additional optimizations not yet executed
- Improved forecasting accuracy
- Future workload growth avoided through better baselines

CHAPTER 16

TURNING OFF SYSTEMS WITHOUT TURNING OFF THE BUSINESS

"Where your attention goes, your time goes."

— IDOWU KOYENIKAN

The hidden cost of "cheap" legacy systems

Legacy systems are often defended with a simple argument: They are already paid for. No new licenses. No new invoices. No immediate pressure to act.

This framing is seductive—and incomplete.

What it overlooks is that systems incur cost by existing, not just by being purchased. They require infrastructure, monitoring, security patching, backup, and operational attention. They introduce dependencies that shape how everything around them must behave.[1]

When legacy platforms persist beyond their functional usefulness, they do not sit quietly. They exert drag on the environment. They slow change. They expand the surface area for risk.

Because these costs are distributed and indirect, they are rarely challenged. "Cheap to keep" becomes a default assumption rather than a measured conclusion.

To understand why organizations tolerate this drag, we must define the before state clearly—not in terms of accounting depreciation but in terms of embedded operational and architectural cost.[2]

[FRAMEWORK STEP 1: DEFINE BEFORE STATE]

Legacy systems are often described as "cheap" because:

- They are fully depreciated
- They still run
- They don't generate new license invoices

But "cheap to keep" is not the same as "free to operate."

In this example, several legacy platforms remained active long after their functional purpose had been replaced. They persisted not because they delivered value but because turning them off felt risky.

The organization carried:

- Redundant systems of record
- Parallel integration paths
- Ongoing operational dependencies

The visible cost looked small.

The before state makes a critical distinction visible: The absence of new invoices does not mean the absence of cost.

Redundant systems carried ongoing operational burden. Parallel paths increased complexity. Dependencies constrained modernization elsewhere. None of these appeared dramatic in isolation, yet together they formed a persistent tax on progress.

Legacy systems were not retained because they delivered value. They were retained because shutting them down felt riskier than leaving them on.

This is how hidden cost survives—not through neglect but through caution.

By naming the embedded cost explicitly, the organization reframes the discussion. The question is no longer, "Why remove something that still works?" It becomes, "Why continue paying for something that no longer contributes?"

Psychological and organizational barriers to shutdown

Decommissioning decisions are rarely blocked by data alone. They are blocked by uncertainty.

Over time, systems outlive the people who designed them. Documentation erodes. Dependencies become implicit rather than explicit. Confidence fades. What remains is a vague sense that something might still rely on the system—even if no one can say what.[3]

This uncertainty produces a powerful bias toward inaction. Keeping a system running feels safe. Turning it off feels irreversible.

Organizationally, responsibility is diffuse. No single group owns the risk end-to-end. As a result, the default decision is to do nothing—indefinitely.

To understand why legacy systems persist, we must acknowledge these human and structural dynamics. The issue is not resistance to change. It is the absence of a safe path forward.[4]

(FRAMEWORK STEPS 3–5: PROCESS STEPS, ACTORS, FREQUENCY)

Actors Identified

- Application Owners
- Infrastructure / Platform Operations
- Security and Compliance
- Business Stakeholders

Before-State Reality

Legacy systems were retained "just in case" due to:

- Uncertainty about downstream dependencies
- Fear of breaking unseen consumers
- Regulatory and audit concerns
- Organizational memory loss

Frequency Captured

- Systems ran **24×7**
- Support effort incurred **continuously**
- Risk exposure persisted **indefinitely**

The decision to keep systems running was rarely revisited—it simply became the default.

This before-state reality explains why "just in case" becomes permanent.

Systems run continuously. Support effort continues quietly. Risk exposure remains open-ended. And because nothing fails visibly, the decision is never revisited.

Inaction hardens into policy.

By capturing frequency and actors, the organization surfaces the true cost of uncertainty. Keeping systems alive is not a one-time choice. It is a recurring decision to accept ongoing cost and risk.

Once this is made explicit, the problem becomes solvable—not through force but through design.

Designing controlled and reversible decommissioning

The breakthrough in this example was not courage. It was reversibility.

By designing decommissioning as a controlled, evidence-driven process, the organization removed the psychological barrier that kept systems running indefinitely. Shutdown no longer meant commitment without recourse.[5]

This reframing changed the question entirely. Instead of asking whether it was safe to turn something off, the organization asked whether it was necessary to keep it on.

Engineering reversibility—through dependency mapping, parallel validation, and rollback plans—transformed risk from an unknown into a managed variable.[6]

This is a design problem, not a persuasion problem. When safety is engineered, behavior follows.

[FRAMEWORK STEP 2: DEFINE AFTER STATE]

The organization reframed shutdown as a **controlled, reversible process**, not a one-way door.

After State Defined (Anonymized)

- Dependency mapping and verification
- Parallel validation of replacement systems
- Controlled read-only periods
- Explicit rollback and recovery plans

Instead of asking: "Can we turn this off?"

The question became: "Can we prove it is safe not to keep it on?"

Risk was not ignored.

It was engineered out systematically.

In the after state, risk was not minimized by avoidance. It was reduced through structure.

By validating dependencies explicitly and preserving rollback options, the organization made decommissioning repeatable and defensible. Decisions were grounded in evidence rather than memory or fear.

Human judgment shifted upward—from guessing about impact to approving controlled outcomes.

This is what allows shutdown to become routine instead of exceptional. When reversibility exists, progress no longer depends on perfect certainty.

Quantifying risk-adjusted savings

Cost savings without risk adjustment are rarely trusted.

Decommissioning initiatives often overpromise by assuming perfect execution and zero remediation. This undermines credibility, even when the underlying logic is sound.

By explicitly pricing risk—and subtracting it from gross savings—the organization produces a defensible, finance-aligned result. This approach acknowledges uncertainty without allowing it to block action.[7]

The goal is not to claim maximum benefit. It is to claim durable benefit.

This is where conservative math strengthens the case rather than weakening it.

(FRAMEWORK STEPS 6 & 9: EFFORT PER STEP, DELTA CALCULATION)

Direct Annual Costs Eliminated

Representative legacy system costs included:

- Infrastructure and hosting: **$40,000/year**
- Licenses and support: **$60,000/year**
- Operational support effort:
    - ~5 hours/week × $120/hour ≈ **$31,200/year**

Total gross annual cost:

$40,000 + $60,000 + $31,200 = $131,200

Risk Adjustment (Explicit)

To remain conservative, the organization applied a **risk discount:**

- Probability of needing rollback or remediation: **25%**
- Expected impact cost if triggered: **$40,000**

Risk-adjusted offset:

0.25 × $40,000 = $10,000

Net Annualized Value

$131,200 – $10,000 = $121,200 per year

This represents **defensible, risk-adjusted savings.**

The resulting figure represents savings that survive scrutiny.

Gross cost is real. Risk is acknowledged. Net value remains material.

By making risk explicit and bounded, the organization replaces vague fear with quantified exposure. Decisions can be made rationally rather than emotionally.

This is how decommissioning moves from opinion to economics—and from debate to execution.

Eliminating "just in case" system retention

Legacy systems almost never exist alone. They accumulate.

Each retained system brings integrations, environments, credentials, monitoring, and support overhead. Over time, these layers reinforce each other, making the environment harder to reason about and more fragile to change.[8]

Applying controlled retirement across multiple systems transforms this dynamic. Complexity stops compounding. Risk surface area shrinks. Support burden declines structurally.

What looks like a single shutdown becomes a pattern of simplification.

This is where decommissioning shifts from tactical savings to architectural progress.

(FRAMEWORK STEPS 7 & 8: SCALE ACROSS TIME, APPLY RATE)

Legacy systems rarely exist in isolation.

When this approach was applied across:

- Multiple applications
- Multiple environments (prod / non-prod)
- Multiple years

The value compounded:

- Each retired system reduced future support burden
- Each dependency removed simplified the environment
- Each shutdown reduced the blast radius of incidents

BUSINESS TRANSLATION

Keeping systems "just in case" is not neutral.

It is a recurring decision to pay for risk you no longer need.

The business reality is straightforward: Keeping systems "just in case" is an active choice, not a neutral default.

Each day they remain live, cost and risk accrue. Each year they persist, complexity hardens.

By eliminating unnecessary retention, the organization stops paying for uncertainty it no longer needs. The environment becomes simpler, safer, and easier to change.

This is how technical debt is retired—not through sweeping programs but through repeatable decisions.

The safe retirement pattern

Patterns endure when they normalize good decisions.

The safe retirement pattern replaces fear-driven retention with evidence-driven simplification. It treats decommissioning as an engineered capability, not a risky exception.[9]

When shutdown is controlled, reversible, and repeatable, systems no longer accumulate by default. The organization gains the ability to subtract—a capability as important as the ability to build.

This pattern applies wherever legacy persists due to uncertainty rather than value.

This pattern changes the economics of the environment.

Savings are real, recurring, and defensible. Risk decreases as complexity recedes. Architecture becomes more intentional over time.[10]

Most importantly, behavior changes. Teams stop keeping systems alive out of fear. They retire them with confidence.

This is not aggressive cost cutting.

It is intentional simplification.

And with this chapter, the framework adds another durable lever:

- Flow (Chapter 10)
- Decision (Chapter 11)
- Awareness (Chapter 12)
- Capacity (Chapter 13)
- Progress (Chapter 14)
- Economics (Chapter 15)
- Complexity reduction (Chapter 16)

Same framework.

Different constraint.

Sustainable value.

Tying it all together

This chapter focuses on a form of value that is often hidden behind caution: the cost of keeping systems alive "just in case."

To make that cost visible, the following example shows how deliberate, evidence-based system retirement translates into measurable business value.

Using a standard value articulation framework, it connects risk-managed decommissioning to hard-dollar savings and reduced operational exposure.

The sections are presented exactly as they would be in practice, illustrating how simplification becomes a defensible business decision rather than a leap of faith.

1. TITLE

Eliminating Recurring Cost and Risk Through Controlled Legacy System Retirement

2. CURRENT SITUATION

(In business terms, what was the gap or the need?)

Several legacy systems remained operational despite having been functionally replaced by modern platforms.

While these systems were stable and fully depreciated, they continued to incur infrastructure, support, and operational overhead.

This created a persistent business gap:

- Ongoing costs for systems no longer delivering material value
- Parallel integrations and dependencies that increased complexity
- Continuous support and security exposure for low-value assets
- Reluctance to decommission due to uncertainty about downstream impact

The issue was not technical failure. It was the absence of confidence to safely turn systems off.

3. OBJECTIVE

(In business terms, what was the business trying to solve?)

The business objective was to reduce unnecessary run cost and risk by retiring obsolete systems without introducing instability or compliance exposure.

Specifically, the organization aimed to:

- Identify and validate true system dependencies
- Eliminate redundant platforms no longer required for operations
- Reduce ongoing support and infrastructure costs
- Replace "just in case" retention with evidence-based decisions

4. SOLUTION

(What was the solution and how did analytics products/services assist?)

A controlled, reversible decommissioning approach was implemented, supported by analytics-driven dependency validation.

Key elements of the solution included:

- Mapping and verification of downstream system dependencies
- Parallel validation of replacement platforms
- Read-only and observation periods prior to shutdown
- Defined rollback procedures to manage residual risk

Analytics products helped surface actual usage patterns and dependency signals, allowing decisions to be based on evidence rather than assumption.

5. BUSINESS VALUE

(Describe the business value in VERY SPECIFIC terms.)

This initiative permanently eliminated the cost of running systems that no longer delivered business value.

As a result:

- Infrastructure and licensing costs were removed from the baseline
- Ongoing operational support effort was eliminated
- Security and operational exposure was reduced
- Architecture complexity decreased, simplifying future change

The value was both financial and structural: **lower run-cost combined with reduced risk and complexity.**

6. BUSINESS VALUE CALCULATION DETAILS

(Describe in very specific terms HOW the business value was calculated.)

To quantify value, the organization calculated the annual cost of operating a representative legacy system and applied a conservative risk adjustment.

Annual Cost Components (Representative):

- Infrastructure and hosting: ~$35,000
- Licensing and vendor support: ~$55,000
- Operational support effort:
  ~4 hours/week × $130/hour ≈ ~$27,000

Gross Annual Cost Eliminated:

- ~$117,000

Risk Adjustment (Conservative):

- Potential remediation or rollback exposure estimated at ~$12,000

Net Annualized Value:

- ~$117,000 – $12,000 ≈ ~$105,000

7. TOTAL AMOUNT OF VALUE FOR THE YEAR (IN $)

≈ $105,000 per year

$105,000 cost avoided in Year 1
$315,000 cost avoided in Year 3

This figure represents **risk-adjusted, recurring savings from retiring a single legacy system.**

It intentionally excludes:

- Reduced incident likelihood
- Simplified future integrations
- Lower long-term security exposure

Those benefits exist but were not monetized to keep the estimate conservative and credible.

CHAPTER 17

GUARDRAILS, NOT GATES: GOVERNANCE THAT SCALES

"Great things in business are never done by one person. They're done by a team of people."

— STEVE JOBS

Governance as a delivery bottleneck

Governance is almost never introduced with the intent to slow delivery. Its purpose is protection—of data, of customers, of the enterprise itself. Yet in many organizations, governance becomes synonymous with delay.

This happens when controls are positioned outside the flow of work. Reviews occur after effort has already begun. Compliance is checked once artifacts exist. Feedback arrives late, often under deadline pressure.[1]

The result is predictable. Delivery teams experience governance as friction. Governance teams experience constant urgency. Neither side believes the system is working as designed.

This is not a failure of policy. It is a failure of placement.

To understand why governance becomes a bottleneck, we must define the before state clearly—not in terms of intent but in terms of how governance interacts with delivery. Only then can we see how protection mechanisms, when misaligned with flow, quietly tax speed, quality, and trust.[2]

[FRAMEWORK STEP 1: DEFINE BEFORE STATE]

Governance is rarely designed to slow teams—but it often does.

In this example, governance controls existed to manage:

- Data access
- Structural standards
- Compliance requirements

However, enforcement relied on **manual review and approval**. Each request passed through one or more governance checkpoints before work could proceed.

The result:

- Delivery queues grew
- Reviews became superficial under pressure
- Teams viewed governance as friction, not protection

Governance existed—but it lived **outside the flow of delivery**.

The before state exposes a fundamental misalignment. Governance existed, but it operated downstream of action.

Because enforcement relied on manual checkpoints, delivery queued behind reviews. Under pressure, reviews became inconsistent. Teams learned to work around governance rather than with it.

The organization paid twice: once for governance effort and again for rework when standards were applied too late.

This is how well-intentioned controls erode credibility. Not because they are wrong but because they arrive after behavior has already formed.

By naming governance as a delivery bottleneck—rather than a cultural problem—the organization creates space for a structural solution.

Cost of inconsistent rule enforcement

Inconsistent enforcement is more expensive than weak enforcement.

When rules are applied unevenly—depending on reviewer, timing, or workload—teams cannot internalize expectations. Instead of building compliance into their work, they wait to be corrected.[3]

This creates a hidden feedback loop. Rework increases. Delivery slows. Audit exposure grows. Governance teams are pulled into repeated clarifications rather than preventive guidance.

To surface this cost, we must look beyond formal policy and examine how rules are enforced in practice: who is involved, how often, and when intervention occurs.

Frequency matters here. Weekly interactions compounded by rework cycles quickly become a material operational burden—even if each individual review feels reasonable in isolation.

(FRAMEWORK STEPS 3–5: PROCESS STEPS, ACTORS, FREQUENCY)

Actors Identified

- Data Governance Team
- Security / Compliance
- Delivery Teams (Engineering, Analytics)

Before-State Process (Mapped)

1. Team submits request for review
2. Governance team evaluates compliance manually
3. Feedback issued, often after work has begun
4. Rework required to meet standards
5. Approval granted retroactively

Frequency Captured

- Governance interactions occurred **weekly**
- Rework introduced **unplanned cycles**
- Enforcement varied by reviewer and timing

Hidden Cost

- Rework effort
- Delayed delivery
- Inconsistent application of policy
- Increased audit exposure due to uneven enforcement

The organization paid twice: once for governance and again for correcting what governance missed.

The mapped process makes the cost visible. Reviews occurred regularly but too late to prevent deviation. Feedback arrived after work had begun, forcing rework and negotiation.

Because enforcement varied, compliance became situational rather than systemic. Risk increased even as effort rose.

This is the paradox of manual governance: More activity does not guarantee better outcomes.

By identifying actors and frequency, the organization reveals why governance felt expensive yet ineffective. The problem was not insufficient control. It was control applied at the wrong point in the flow.

Embedding policy directly into delivery flow

Preventative governance requires a different design philosophy.

Instead of asking people to remember rules and apply them under pressure, the system itself must shape behavior. Policy must move upstream—into the moment where decisions are made and actions are taken.

Embedding governance into delivery flow does not remove human oversight. It changes where that oversight is applied. Automation handles the predictable cases. Humans focus on ambiguity and true exceptions.[4]

This reframing turns governance from a gate into a guide. Instead of slowing delivery after the fact, it influences outcomes before they occur.[5]

Defining the after state at this level makes clear that effective governance is not heavier. It is earlier.

[FRAMEWORK STEP 2: DEFINE AFTER STATE]

The organization reframed governance as **preventive**, not reactive.

After State Defined (Anonymized)

- Policies translated into executable rules
- Controls embedded directly into development and data workflows
- Violations blocked or flagged *before* delivery
- Manual review reserved for true exceptions

Instead of gating progress after the fact, governance **shaped behavior at the moment of action.**

Human oversight remained—but it was applied where judgment mattered.

In the after state, compliance is no longer something teams achieve through negotiation. It is something they inherit by default.

Because rules are executable and embedded, violations are prevented or flagged immediately. Rework collapses. Consistency increases.

Human review becomes more valuable, not less. Time is spent on judgment, not repetition.

This is the structural shift that allows governance to coexist with speed—not by compromising standards but by enforcing them where they matter most.

Measuring risk reduction without incidents

Governance is often justified by the disasters it prevents—breaches, audit findings, regulatory penalties. Yet relying on incidents to prove value creates a paradox: Success looks like nothing happened.[6]

This makes governance difficult to quantify. When controls work, there is no visible event to measure.

By focusing on effort avoided and consistency gained, the organization quantifies governance value without waiting for failure. This approach aligns with how risk is actually managed—through probability reduction, not incident count.[7]

Conservative assumptions matter here. The goal is not to inflate impact, but to establish credibility.

[FRAMEWORK STEPS 6 & 9: EFFORT PER STEP, DELTA CALCULATION]

Governance value often shows up as **what does not happen.**

Before-State Governance Cost

- Manual review effort:
  - ~10 governance reviews per week
  - ~2 hours per review
  - **20 hours/week**

After-State Governance Cost

- Automated enforcement for standard cases
- Manual review required for ~20% of requests
- ~4 hours/week of governance effort

Effort Delta

20 – 4 = 16 hours/week avoided

Annualized Effort Avoided

16 × 52 = 832 hours/year

Blended Rate Assumption

- Governance, security, and senior engineering roles
- **$140/hour fully loaded**

Direct Annual Value

832 × $140 = $116,480 per year

This calculation includes **only effort avoided.**

Risk Reduction (Conservative)

- Reduced likelihood of non-compliant delivery
- Lower probability of audit findings
- Fewer late-stage remediation events

These benefits are acknowledged but **not monetized** to remain conservative.

The effort delta provides a concrete, defensible baseline. Fewer manual reviews. Less coordination. More consistent outcomes.

The excluded benefits—fewer incidents, lower audit exposure, reduced remediation—are real but intentionally unpriced. Their omission strengthens the claim.

This is how governance value can be measured responsibly: by quantifying what disappears when prevention works.

Scaling compliance with minimal marginal cost

Manual governance does not scale gracefully.

Each new team increases review volume. Each additional delivery introduces delay. Cost and coordination rise together.

Embedded governance behaves differently. Once controls are in place, scale becomes an advantage. New teams inherit guardrails automatically. Enforcement remains consistent regardless of volume.[8]

This is where governance transitions from overhead to infrastructure.

By examining how compliance scales, the organization reveals the long-term economics of control—not just its short-term cost.

(FRAMEWORK STEPS 7 & 8: SCALE ACROSS TIME, APPLY RATE)

Manual governance scales linearly:

- More teams → more reviews → more delay

Embedded governance scales sub-linearly:

- New teams inherit controls automatically
- Enforcement consistency increases
- Marginal cost approaches zero

BUSINESS TRANSLATION

Every additional delivery:

- Costs less to govern
- Carries less risk
- Requires less coordination

This is where governance stops being overhead and becomes **infrastructure.**

The business reality is decisive. When governance is embedded, marginal cost approaches zero while protection increases.

Delivery accelerates because compliance is predictable. Risk decreases because enforcement is consistent. Coordination overhead collapses.

Governance stops being something teams navigate. It becomes something they rely on.

This is the point at which governance earns trust.

The guardrails pattern

Patterns endure when they resolve false tradeoffs.

The guardrails pattern eliminates the perceived tension between speed and control. By embedding rules into flow, organizations achieve both.[9]

Compliance becomes the default behavior. Governance effort concentrates where judgment is required. Friction disappears without standards eroding.

This pattern applies anywhere rules exist but are enforced too late to be effective.

The guardrails pattern changes how organizations experience governance.

Delivery becomes faster, not slower. Compliance becomes more reliable, not more negotiable. Risk decreases without adding bureaucracy.[10]

Most importantly, behavior changes. Teams stop treating governance as an obstacle and start trusting it as protection.

This is not lighter governance.

It is governance that finally works.

And with this chapter, the framework closes another misconception:

- Cost alignment (Chapter 15)
- Risk-adjusted simplification (Chapter 16)
- Prevention without paralysis (Chapter 17)

Same framework.

Different misconception removed.

Structural value sustained.

Tying it all together

This chapter reframes governance from a control mechanism into a delivery accelerator.

To make that shift tangible, the following example shows how embedding policy directly into workflows produces measurable business value.

Using a standard value articulation framework, it connects preventative governance to reduced effort, faster delivery, and lower risk exposure.

The sections are presented exactly as they would be in practice, illustrating how compliance can scale without scaling bureaucracy.

1. TITLE

Reducing Governance Effort and Delivery Friction Through Embedded Controls

2. CURRENT SITUATION

(In business terms, what was the gap or the need?)

Governance controls existed to manage data access, standards, and compliance, but enforcement relied heavily on manual review and approval. Delivery teams frequently encountered governance late in the process, after work had already begun.

This created a recurring business gap:

- Delivery delays caused by review queues
- Rework required to address issues discovered late
- Inconsistent enforcement of standards across teams
- Friction between governance functions and delivery teams

The issue was not lack of governance. It was that governance lived outside the flow of delivery.

3. OBJECTIVE

(In business terms, what was the business trying to solve?)

The business objective was to reduce governance-related friction and risk without weakening controls or slowing delivery.

Specifically, the organization aimed to:

- Enforce standards consistently and early
- Reduce manual review effort for routine requests
- Minimize rework caused by late-stage compliance findings
- Allow governance to scale as delivery volume increased

4. SOLUTION

(What was the solution and how did analytics products/services assist?)

Governance policies were translated into executable rules and embedded directly into delivery workflows.

Key elements of the solution included:

- Automated enforcement of structural and access standards
- Pre-deployment checks to prevent non-compliant changes
- Exception-based workflows for cases requiring human judgment
- Monitoring and reporting to validate adherence over time

Analytics products enabled governance teams to shift from reviewing work to designing and monitoring rules.

5. BUSINESS VALUE

(Describe the business value in VERY SPECIFIC terms.)

This initiative significantly reduced the effort required to govern delivery while improving consistency.

As a result:

- The majority of requests passed through governance without manual review
- Delivery teams experienced fewer delays and less rework
- Governance effort focused on true exceptions rather than routine cases
- Compliance became predictable instead of negotiable

The core value was structural: lower marginal cost of governance as delivery volume increased.

6. BUSINESS VALUE CALCULATION DETAILS

(Describe in very specific terms HOW the business value was calculated.)

To quantify value, the organization measured governance effort before and after embedding controls.

Assumptions (Conservative):

- Governance reviews before automation: ~10 per week
- Average effort per review: ~2 hours
- Total manual governance effort before: ~20 hours/week

After Embedded Governance:

- Manual reviews required for ~20% of cases
- Average manual effort after: ~4 hours/week

Annual Effort Avoided:

- (20 – 4) hours/week × 52 weeks = ~832 hours per year

Blended Fully Loaded Rate:

- Governance, security, and senior engineering roles: ~$145/hour

7. TOTAL AMOUNT OF VALUE FOR THE YEAR (IN $)

832 hours × $145/hour ≈ ~$121,000 per year

$121,000 cost avoided in Year 1

$363,000 cost avoided in Year 3

This figure reflects direct labor efficiency from reduced manual governance effort.

It intentionally excludes:

- Avoided audit findings
- Reduced incident remediation
- Faster time-to-market from fewer delays

Those benefits exist but were not monetized to keep the estimate conservative and defensible.

CHAPTER 18

SEPARATING SIGNAL FROM NOISE AT OPERATIONAL SCALE

"Continuous effort, not strength or intelligence, is the key to unlocking our potential."

— WINSTON CHURCHILL

Decision degradation caused by data overload

Modern systems excel at producing information. Metrics, alerts, dashboards, and notifications flow continuously. What they rarely produce is judgment.

As organizations instrument more of their operations, signal volume increases faster than decision capacity. Leaders and operators are exposed to more data than they can meaningfully process. The assumption is that more visibility leads to better outcomes.[1]

In practice, the opposite often occurs.

When everything is flagged, nothing stands out. Attention fragments. Important signals blend into background noise. Over time, teams adapt by scanning, skimming, or ignoring alerts altogether.[2]

This is not negligence. It is a rational response to overload.

To understand how decision quality degrades, we must define the before state clearly—not in terms of data availability but in terms of cognitive burden. Only then can we see how technically correct information can still undermine effective decision-making.

[FRAMEWORK STEP 1: DEFINE BEFORE STATE]

Operational systems are very good at producing data.

They are far less good at producing **clarity**.

In this example, leaders and operators were inundated with:

- Alerts
- Reports
- Variance notifications
- Dashboard indicators

Most of these signals were technically correct—but operationally irrelevant.

As volume increased, a predictable degradation occurred:

- Important signals were missed
- Teams stopped trusting alerts
- Decisions slowed or defaulted to habit

This is not a data problem.

It is **decision degradation caused by noise.**

The before state reveals a paradox: visibility increased, but clarity declined.

Signals were abundant, accurate, and well-intentioned—yet they failed to guide action. As volume grew, trust eroded. Alerts lost meaning. Decisions defaulted to habit rather than evidence.

This is how decision degradation occurs. Not through lack of data but through excess of it.

By naming noise as the problem, the organization reframes the challenge. The goal is no longer to generate more insight but to restore discernment.

Manual triage as hidden operational labor

When systems cannot distinguish signal from noise, humans are forced to compensate.[3]

Manual triage becomes the hidden labor of overloaded environments. Analysts, managers, and on-call staff spend significant portions of their day reviewing alerts, dismissing non-issues, and confirming that nothing requires action.

This effort is rarely tracked because it feels like vigilance rather than work. Yet it consumes attention continuously and delays response to genuine issues.

To make this cost visible, we must map the process as it actually occurs and capture its frequency. Daily repetition transforms small tasks into material effort.[4]

What appears to be situational monitoring becomes a structural drain on capacity.

(FRAMEWORK STEPS 3–5: PROCESS STEPS, ACTORS, FREQUENCY)

Actors Identified

- Operations Analysts
- Managers
- On-call Support Roles

Before-State Process (Mapped)

1. Alerts and reports generated automatically
2. Humans reviewed large volumes of notifications
3. Non-actionable items dismissed manually
4. True issues escalated after review
5. Follow-up initiated, often late

Frequency Captured (Explicit)

- Alerts reviewed **daily**
- Volume per analyst: **40–60 signals per day**
- True actionable items: **~10–15%**

Most effort was spent proving that **nothing needed to be done.**

The mapped process shows where effort truly went. Most time was not spent resolving problems but proving their absence.

Because review happened after alerts were generated, human attention was consumed upstream of action. True issues surfaced only after triage completed—often later than optimal.

This is the cost of noise: effort without progress.

By identifying actors and frequency, the organization surfaces a form of operational labor that is almost never budgeted, yet widely experienced.

Designing systems for exceptions, not volume

Attention is finite. Systems that ignore this fact eventually fail their users.

The shift in this example was not technical sophistication but design intent. Instead of maximizing information output, the organization optimized for human engagement at the right moments.

Designing for exceptions requires clarity about decision thresholds. What actually requires action? What can safely be ignored? What should be suppressed entirely?

By embedding these distinctions into the system, information volume collapses without reducing awareness. Humans are no longer asked to filter noise. They are engaged only when judgment is required.[5, 6]

This is a system-level respect for cognitive limits—and a prerequisite for sustained decision quality.

[FRAMEWORK STEP 2: DEFINE AFTER STATE]

The organization reframed the goal:

Reduce human attention, not increase information.

After State Defined (Anonymized)

- Rules-based thresholds aligned to decision points
- Exception-driven alerting models
- Automated suppression of low-value noise
- Escalation only when action was required

Instead of reviewing *everything*, humans were engaged **only when it mattered.**

Attention became a scarce resource—and the system treated it that way.

In the after state, attention became intentional.

Alerts were no longer invitations to review but prompts to act. Low-value noise disappeared. Escalation aligned with decision points.

Human effort did not increase. It focused.

This is the defining shift: Systems stopped asking people to compensate for poor signal design and began protecting attention as a critical resource.

Speed and quality gains through subtraction

Improvement is often associated with addition—more dashboards, more indicators, more automation.

In this case, improvement came through subtraction.

By reducing the number of alerts humans were asked to process, the organization reclaimed time and focus simultaneously. Fewer signals meant faster interpretation. Fewer interruptions meant better judgment.[7]

Measuring effort per day before and after makes this impact tangible. It captures the benefit of removing work that never should have existed.[8]

This is where clarity becomes measurable.

(FRAMEWORK STEPS 6 & 9: EFFORT PER STEP, DELTA CALCULATION)

Effort per Day (Before)

- ~50 alerts reviewed per analyst
- ~2 minutes per alert

$50 \times 2 = 100$ minutes/day

Effort per Day (After)

- ~8 exception alerts per analyst
- ~3 minutes per alert

$8 \times 3 = 24$ minutes/day

Net Effort Delta

$100 - 24 = 76$ minutes/day

Annualized Effort Avoided

Assumptions:

- 1 analyst
- 240 working days/year

76 minutes $\times 240 = 18{,}240$ minutes
$18{,}240 \div 60 \approx 304$ hours/year

The effort delta is straightforward and defensible. Time previously spent scanning was redirected to action.

Importantly, effort per alert increased slightly—because remaining alerts mattered. This is a positive outcome. Attention was no longer diluted.

The result is faster response with higher confidence—not because people worked harder but because the system worked smarter.

Improved decision outcomes through signal clarity

The most important outcome of signal reduction is not time saved. It is trust restored.

When alerts fire rarely and meaningfully, teams respond differently. They believe the signal. They act without hesitation. Decisions move closer to events.[9]

By applying a blended rate, the organization grounds this improvement in economic terms without overstating impact. Only direct effort reduction is claimed.

The behavioral effects—faster response, fewer errors, better decisions—are acknowledged but intentionally not monetized. Their value is real, but their exclusion preserves credibility.[10]

(FRAMEWORK STEPS 7 & 8: SCALE ACROSS TIME, APPLY RATE)

Blended Rate Assumption

- Operations analysts and managers
- Fully loaded rate: **$130/hour**

Direct Annualized Value

304 hours × $130/hour = $39,520 per year (per analyst)

This calculation includes **only**:

- Reduced manual triage effort

It explicitly excludes:

- Faster incident response
- Reduced operational errors
- Better managerial decisions

Those benefits exist but are not monetized here.

Behavioral Impact (Qualitative, not Monetized)

- Alerts are trusted again
- Decisions happen faster
- Important signals are not ignored

This is where **quality improves because volume decreases.**

The calculated savings are modest—and persistent.

More importantly, decision behavior changed. Alerts were trusted again. Noise no longer masked risk. Attention was applied deliberately.

By restoring clarity, the organization created conditions for better decisions without adding complexity or cost.

The signal extraction pattern

Patterns endure when they resolve systemic failure modes.

The signal extraction pattern addresses a fundamental limitation of modern operations: Human attention does not scale with data volume.[11]

By designing systems that surface only what requires action, organizations protect decision quality as complexity increases.

This pattern applies wherever alerts, reports, or dashboards overwhelm their intended audience.

[FRAMEWORK STEP 10: TRANSLATE INTO BUSINESS LANGUAGE]

This example demonstrates a reusable pattern:

When systems respect human attention, decision quality improves and effort collapses.

BUSINESS TRANSLATION

This initiative delivered:

- Measurable labor savings from reduced triage
- Faster response to real issues
- Higher confidence in operational signals

More importantly, it changed behavior:

- Teams stopped scanning and started acting
- Noise no longer masked risk
- Attention was applied where it mattered

This is not better reporting.

It is **decision enablement at scale.**

The signal extraction pattern changes how decisions are made.

Effort collapses because triage disappears. Speed increases because relevance is assured. Confidence returns because signals can be trusted.

Most importantly, behavior changes. Teams stop scanning and start acting.

This is not better reporting.

It is decision enablement at scale.

And with this chapter, the framework completes another critical dimension:

- Flow (Chapter 10)
- Decision latency (Chapter 11)
- Awareness (Chapter 12)
- Capacity (Chapter 13)
- Progress (Chapter 14)
- Economics (Chapter 15)
- Complexity reduction (Chapter 16)
- Attention management (Chapter 17)

Same framework.

Different failure mode.

Enduring clarity.

Tying it all together

This chapter focuses on a subtle but costly problem: when too much information competes for limited human attention.

To translate that concept into measurable value, the following example shows how reducing operational noise creates real, quantifiable impact.

Using a standard business value framework, it connects exception-based visibility to reduced effort and faster, higher-quality decisions.

The sections are presented exactly as they would be in practice, illustrating how clarity itself becomes a defensible business asset.

1. TITLE

Reducing Operational Effort by Shifting from Volume-Based Alerts to Exception Signals

2. CURRENT SITUATION

(In business terms, what was the gap or the need?)

Operational teams were supported by dashboards, alerts, and reports designed to surface system and performance issues. While technically accurate, these signals were generated at high volume and required human review to determine relevance.

This created a persistent business gap:

- Analysts and managers reviewed large numbers of non-actionable alerts
- Significant time was spent confirming that no action was required
- Important signals were occasionally missed due to alert fatigue
- Decision speed degraded as attention was spread thin

The issue was not lack of data—it was that attention was consumed faster than it could be replenished.

3. OBJECTIVE

(In business terms, what was the business trying to solve?)

The business objective was to reduce the amount of human effort spent reviewing low-value information while improving the speed and quality of operational decisions.

Specifically, the organization aimed to:

- Suppress non-actionable signals automatically
- Surface only exceptions that required intervention
- Reduce manual triage effort without increasing risk
- Restore trust in alerts and operational indicators

4. SOLUTION

(What was the solution and how did analytics products/ services assist?)

An exception-driven monitoring approach was implemented supported by analytics-based thresholds and suppression logic.

Key elements of the solution included:

- Definition of decision-relevant thresholds aligned to action points
- Automated suppression of signals within normal operating ranges
- Escalation logic that surfaced only true exceptions
- Centralized views focused on issues requiring response

Analytics products enabled the system to respect human attention by filtering noise before it reached decision-makers.

5. BUSINESS VALUE

(Describe the business value in VERY SPECIFIC terms.)

This initiative significantly reduced the daily effort required to monitor operations.

As a result:

- Analysts reviewed far fewer alerts per day
- Time spent dismissing non-issues was largely eliminated
- True issues were identified and acted on more quickly
- Decision confidence increased as signal quality improved

The core value was not better dashboards—it was **less cognitive load applied to the same operational scope.**

6. BUSINESS VALUE CALCULATION DETAILS

(Describe in very specific terms HOW the business value was calculated.)

To quantify value, the organization compared analyst effort spent on alert review before and after exception-based filtering.

Assumptions (Conservative):

- Alerts reviewed per analyst per day before: ~45
- Average review time per alert: ~2 minutes
- Daily effort before: ~90 minutes

After Exception-Based Filtering:

- Alerts reviewed per day: ~8
- Average review time per alert: ~3 minutes
- Daily effort after: ~24 minutes

Net Effort Avoided per Day:

- ~66 minutes

Annual Effort Avoided:

- 66 minutes × 240 working days ≈ ~264 hours per year

Blended Fully Loaded Rate:

- Operations analysts and managers: ~$135/hour

7. TOTAL AMOUNT OF VALUE FOR THE YEAR (IN $)

264 hours × $135/hour ≈ ~$35,600 per year (per analyst)

$35,600 cost avoided in Year 1
$106,800 cost avoided in Year 3

This figure reflects **direct labor efficiency from reduced manual triage effort.**

It intentionally excludes:

- Faster incident resolution
- Avoided operational errors
- Improved managerial decision quality

Those benefits exist but were not monetized to keep the estimate conservative and defensible.

CHAPTER 19

DESIGNING ASSETS THAT OUTLIVE THE PROJECT

"Business is all about solving people's problems—at a profit."

— PAUL MARSEN

Why delivered projects fail to sustain value

Most data and analytics initiatives are judged by delivery, not durability.

Projects are scoped, funded, and celebrated when outputs go live. Dashboards launch. Models are approved. Reports circulate. On paper, success is achieved.[1]

Yet value persistence is rarely examined.

When delivery is optimized for completion rather than continuity, insight decays quietly. What was built for one initiative fails to serve the next. Teams start over, often unknowingly recreating logic that already exists elsewhere.

This is not because teams forget. It is because the system does not remember.

To understand why value fails to sustain, we must define the before state in terms of delivery economics—not whether projects succeed once but whether what they produce can be reused. Without that lens, organizations mistake motion for momentum.[2]

[FRAMEWORK STEP 1: DEFINE BEFORE STATE]

Most data and analytics initiatives succeed once—and then quietly lose value.

In this example, the organization delivered analytics and data solutions through discrete projects. Each project met its immediate objective, but little of what was built carried forward intact.

Common symptoms included:

- Logic rebuilt for similar use cases
- Slightly different definitions for the same metrics
- Teams repeating discovery and modeling work
- Knowledge leaving with project members

Value was delivered—but it decayed immediately after go-live.

The before state reveals a subtle but costly pattern: value reset.

Each project delivered something useful but nothing durable. Logic lived inside artifacts. Knowledge lived inside people. When the project ended, both dispersed.

This forced teams to relearn, rebuild, and revalidate—even when problems were familiar. Effort repeated. Definitions drifted. Trust eroded.

The organization did not lack talent or discipline. It lacked a delivery model designed to compound value.

By naming this explicitly, the problem shifts from execution quality to structural design. The issue is not how well projects are delivered. It is what survives them.

Assets versus disposable outputs

The distinction between outputs and assets is subtle—and decisive.[3]

Outputs are designed to answer a question. Assets are designed to answer many. Outputs satisfy immediate demand. Assets persist, evolve, and serve future needs.

Most project-based delivery models optimize for outputs. Logic is embedded in reports. Models are shaped around a single use case. Documentation is minimal because the work is "done."

When similar requests arise, teams do not reuse. They reconstruct.

To expose the cost of this model, we must examine how work flows from project to project and how often similar logic is recreated. Frequency matters here. Monthly initiatives with overlapping needs turn disposability into structural inefficiency.[4]

(FRAMEWORK STEPS 3–5: PROCESS STEPS, ACTORS, FREQUENCY)

Actors Identified

- Analytics Engineers
- Data Modelers
- Product and Business Analysts
- Platform Teams

Before-State Delivery Model (Mapped)

1. Project-specific requirements defined
2. Custom logic and models built
3. Outputs delivered (dashboards, datasets, reports)
4. Minimal abstraction or documentation
5. Next project starts from scratch

Frequency Captured

- New initiatives launched **monthly**
- Many requests overlapped in structure or logic
- Reuse occurred informally, if at all

The organization produced **outputs**, not assets.

Outputs satisfy a moment.

Assets persist.

The mapped delivery model explains why reuse was rare. Nothing was designed to survive beyond its immediate context.

Because abstraction was minimal and ownership unclear, reuse required effort and trust. Informal copying replaced deliberate reuse. Variations accumulated.

The organization was productive—but not compounding.

By making the asset-versus-output distinction explicit, the organization surfaces the true constraint. Value was delivered repeatedly but never accumulated.

Designing for reuse beyond first implementation

Designing for reuse requires intent.

It means accepting slightly higher upfront effort to avoid repeated downstream cost. It means prioritizing clarity and consistency over speed and customization.

This is a strategic choice, not a technical one.

By reframing delivery around durable assets, the organization changed what "done" meant. Completion was no longer defined by go-live but by whether future teams could extend what was built without starting over.[5]

This required canonical models, standardized patterns, and clear ownership—not to constrain creativity but to channel it productively.

The after state reflects a shift in optimization: from minimizing initial delivery time to minimizing lifetime cost.[6]

[FRAMEWORK STEP 2: DEFINE AFTER STATE]

The organization reframed delivery around **durable assets**, not project artifacts.

After State Defined (Anonymized)

- Canonical data models for core domains
- Standardized calculation patterns
- Shared transformation logic with clear ownership
- Versioned assets designed for extension

Design decisions prioritized:

- Clarity over speed
- Reusability over customization
- Long-term cost over short-term delivery optics

The goal was not to move slower. It was to **never rebuild the same thing twice.**

In the after state, reuse became intentional rather than accidental.

Assets were designed to be extended. Logic was versioned instead of copied. Knowledge was encoded rather than implied.

This did not slow delivery over time. It accelerated it—because the second and third implementations were dramatically cheaper than the first.

This is how organizations escape the rebuild cycle. Not by working harder but by designing once for many uses.

Compounding returns from repeated reuse

The economics of reuse are backloaded.

The first implementation often costs slightly more. The second costs far less. Each subsequent reuse increases the return without requiring proportional effort.

This is why reuse is difficult to justify without explicit measurement. Its value does not appear immediately. It compounds quietly as frequency increases.

By quantifying effort per initiative before and after, the organization makes this compounding visible. The math is intentionally conservative, focusing on avoided rebuild effort rather than downstream benefits.[7]

This is where asset thinking translates into arithmetic.

(FRAMEWORK STEPS 6 & 9: EFFORT PER STEP, DELTA CALCULATION)

The value of reuse appears after the first project.

Effort per Initiative (Before)

- Rebuilding common models and logic: **~80 hours per project**

Effort per Initiative (After)

- Initial build (first use): **~100 hours**
- Subsequent reuse: **~20 hours per project**

Net Effort Avoided Per Reuse
80 – 20 = 60 hours avoided

Frequency of Reuse (Explicit Assumption)

- Reused across **6 subsequent initiatives per year**

Annual Effort Avoided
60 hours × 6 = 360 hours/year

This calculation reflects **one reusable asset.**

Most organizations create many.

The calculated effort avoided reflects only one asset reused across a handful of initiatives. Even at that scale, the impact is material.

As assets accumulate, the effect multiplies. Each additional reuse lowers average delivery cost. Each extension reinforces consistency.

This is how value compounds without additional headcount. The system remembers what the organization has already learned.

Institutional memory as a system capability

Organizations often rely on people to carry institutional memory.

Over time, this becomes fragile. Turnover occurs. Context fades. Decisions lose rationale. Teams unknowingly repeat past work.

By encoding knowledge into shared, reusable assets, the organization shifts memory from individuals to systems. Definitions persist. Patterns endure. Trust stabilizes.

Applying a blended rate translates this capability into economic terms without overstating impact. Only avoided rebuild effort is priced. The broader benefits—faster onboarding, fewer errors, stronger adoption—are acknowledged but excluded.[8]

This conservatism strengthens the claim.

[FRAMEWORK STEPS 7 & 8: SCALE ACROSS TIME, APPLY RATE]

Blended Rate Assumption

- Senior analytics and data engineering roles
- Fully loaded rate: **$150/hour**

Direct Annualized Value (Per Asset)

360 hours × $150/hour = $54,000 per year

Why This Is Conservative

This calculation excludes:

- Faster onboarding of new team members
- Reduced errors from consistent definitions
- Improved trust and adoption
- Cross-team acceleration

It monetizes **only avoided rebuild effort.**

Over time, assets accumulate. So does value.

This is institutional memory encoded in systems, not people.

The resulting value is recurring and cumulative. Each year the same assets prevent the same rebuilds.

More importantly, they prevent drift. Definitions remain aligned. Models evolve coherently. New team members inherit understanding rather than reconstruct it.

This is institutional memory made durable—not through documentation alone, but through executable structure.

The durable asset pattern

Patterns endure when they change delivery economics.

The durable asset pattern reframes analytics and data work as long-lived infrastructure rather than disposable output. It recognizes that most questions are variations on familiar themes.[9]

When assets are designed for reuse, marginal delivery cost approaches zero. Each new initiative builds on what already exists.[10]

This pattern applies wherever projects repeat similar logic under different names.

(FRAMEWORK STEP 10: TRANSLATE INTO BUSINESS LANGUAGE)

This example demonstrates a powerful enterprise pattern:

When organizations invest once and reuse deliberately, marginal delivery cost approaches zero.

BUSINESS TRANSLATION

This initiative delivered:

- **Recurring labor savings** through avoided rebuilds
- **Consistency across initiatives**
- **Reduced dependency on individual knowledge holders**

Most importantly, it changed delivery economics:

- Each new initiative became cheaper than the last
- Knowledge persisted beyond projects and people
- Value compounded instead of resetting

This is not efficiency. It is **structural leverage.**

The durable asset pattern changes how value behaves over time.

Delivery becomes cheaper, faster, and more consistent with each iteration. Knowledge persists beyond projects and people. Trust increases because results align.

This is not efficiency.

It is structural leverage.

And with this chapter, the framework reaches another inflection point:

- Flow (Chapter 10)
- Decision latency (Chapter 11)
- Awareness (Chapter 12)
- Capacity (Chapter 13)
- Progress (Chapter 14)
- Economics (Chapter 15)
- Complexity reduction (Chapter 16)
- Attention management (Chapter 17)
- Value persistence (Chapter 18)

Same framework.
Different failure mode.
Compounding value.

Tying it all together

This chapter shifts the focus from delivering outputs to creating assets that persist.

To make that distinction concrete, the following example shows how designing for reuse translates into measurable, recurring business value.

Using a standard value articulation framework, it connects reusable data and analytics assets to reduced effort and compounding returns over time.

The sections are presented exactly as they would be in practice, illustrating how institutional memory becomes an economic advantage.

1. TITLE

Reducing Delivery Effort Through Reusable Analytics and Data Assets

2. CURRENT SITUATION

(In business terms, what was the gap or the need?)

Analytics and data solutions were delivered through discrete projects that met their immediate objectives but did not carry forward in a reusable form. Each new initiative required teams to rediscover requirements, rebuild logic, and recreate similar models.

This created a recurring business gap:

- Similar logic was rebuilt across multiple initiatives
- Definitions varied slightly between projects
- Delivery effort reset with each new request
- Knowledge walked out the door when team members changed

Value was delivered once—then decayed.

3. OBJECTIVE

(In business terms, what was the business trying to solve?)

The business objective was to reduce repeated delivery effort by designing analytics and data solutions as reusable assets rather than one-off project outputs.

Specifically, the organization aimed to:

- Standardize core models and calculations
- Enable reuse across multiple initiatives
- Reduce effort required for subsequent implementations
- Lower the marginal cost of each new analytics request

4. SOLUTION

(What was the solution and how did analytics products/services assist?)

Delivery was restructured around durable, versioned assets designed for extension and reuse.

Key elements of the solution included:

- Canonical data models for core business domains
- Standardized calculation and transformation patterns
- Shared assets with clear ownership and documentation
- Versioning practices that supported evolution without rebuild

Analytics products enabled teams to assemble solutions from existing components rather than starting from scratch.

5. BUSINESS VALUE

(Describe the business value in VERY SPECIFIC terms.)

This initiative reduced the effort required to deliver analytics across multiple initiatives.

As a result:

- Subsequent projects reused existing models and logic
- Delivery time decreased after the first implementation
- Consistency improved across analytics outputs
- Teams avoided rebuilding common components repeatedly

The most important outcome was structural: **Each new initiative became cheaper than the last.**

6. BUSINESS VALUE CALCULATION DETAILS

(Describe in very specific terms HOW the business value was calculated.)

To quantify value, the organization measured effort required to deliver analytics before and after asset reuse.

Assumptions (Conservative):

- Initial asset creation effort: ~100 hours
- Effort to reuse and extend asset: ~20 hours per initiative
- Effort avoided per reuse: ~60 hours
- Number of reuse instances per year: ~6

Annual Effort Avoided:

- 60 hours × 6 initiatives = 360 hours per year

Blended Fully Loaded Rate:

- Senior analytics and data engineering roles: ~$150/hour

7. TOTAL AMOUNT OF VALUE FOR THE YEAR (IN $)

360 hours × \$150/hour = ~\$54,000 per year (per reusable asset)

\$54,000 in cost avoided in Year 1
\$162,000 in cost avoided in Year 3

This figure reflects **direct labor savings from avoided rebuild effort.**

It intentionally excludes:

- Faster onboarding of new team members
- Reduced error rates from consistent definitions
- Increased trust and adoption

Those benefits exist but were not monetized to keep the estimate conservative and defensible.

CHAPTER 20

SHIFTING FAILURE LEFT BEFORE THE BUSINESS FEELS IT

"The only real mistake is the one from which we learn nothing."

— HENRY FORD

The cost of late-stage failure

Most operational failures are not sudden. They are delayed.

Small defects enter systems quietly, often during routine change. At the moment of introduction, their impact is negligible. Nothing breaks. No alarms sound. Work continues.[1]

The cost emerges later—when those defects propagate into downstream processes that assume correctness. By the time symptoms appear, the failure has expanded beyond its point of origin. Multiple teams are involved. Decisions are delayed. Corrections are rushed.

This is why late-stage failure is so expensive. It is not the defect itself that drives cost. It is the blast radius created by delayed detection.

To understand this dynamic, we must define the before state precisely—not by the severity of incidents but by when failures are discovered. Timing, not intent, determines impact.[2]

[FRAMEWORK STEP 1: DEFINE BEFORE STATE]

Most operational failures do not begin as incidents. They begin as **small defects introduced quietly upstream.**

In this example, data and operational issues routinely entered the environment during:

- Data ingestion
- Transformation logic changes
- Schema evolution
- Integration updates

These defects were rarely catastrophic at first.

They became expensive only because they were **detected late**—after downstream systems and business processes had already consumed them.

The organization experienced:

- Firefighting during reporting cycles
- Last-minute corrections
- Emergency coordination across teams

The cost was not just fixing the issue. It was **absorbing the blast radius.**

The before state reveals a familiar pattern: Defects were inevitable but containment was not.

Because issues surfaced only after consumption, response required coordination across teams under time pressure. Firefighting replaced diagnosis. Temporary fixes replaced durable correction.

This is how operational fragility develops—not through poor engineering but through late awareness.

By naming late-stage failure as the true cost driver, the organization reframes quality. The problem is not that issues exist. It is that they are allowed to travel too far before being seen.

Early origins of operational failure

Failures often appear to originate downstream because that is where they are felt.

Reports break. Metrics drift. Plans misalign. Yet the root cause almost always lies upstream—in ingestion, transformation, schema change, or integration logic.

When detection is indirect, investigation becomes reactive. Teams chase symptoms instead of sources. Time is spent tracing impact rather than preventing it.

To surface this cost, we must map the actual failure path: who introduces change, how issues surface, and how often escalation occurs. Frequency matters here. Weekly defects that escalate monthly represent accumulated exposure, not isolated mistakes.

This is where quality problems reveal their true shape—not as rare catastrophes but as repeated, delayed discoveries.[3]

(FRAMEWORK STEPS 3–5: PROCESS STEPS, ACTORS, FREQUENCY)

Actors Identified

- Data Engineers
- Analytics Engineers
- Platform Operations
- Business Stakeholders (downstream impact)

Before-State Process (Mapped)

1. Changes deployed to pipelines or logic
2. Issues surfaced indirectly via downstream anomalies
3. Investigation triggered reactively
4. Multiple teams engaged to diagnose impact
5. Corrections applied under time pressure

Frequency Captured

- Minor defects introduced **weekly**
- Material downstream impact observed **monthly**
- Escalations clustered around reporting or planning cycles

Failures were detected—but only after the business felt them.

The mapped process shows why response was so disruptive. Detection occurred only after downstream impact, pulling multiple teams into diagnosis and recovery.

Because escalation clustered around critical cycles, stress was amplified. Work became urgent precisely when accuracy mattered most.

Failures were detected—but too late to be cheap.

By identifying actors and frequency, the organization makes visible the compounding cost of delayed awareness. What felt like episodic incidents was actually a systemic timing problem.

Automated detection before failure becomes impact

The turning point in this example was not eliminating defects. It was collapsing the detection window.

By reframing quality as early detection, the organization shifted its focus from correction to containment. The objective was no longer to prevent all failure—an impossible goal—but to ensure that failure was discovered before it propagated.

Embedding validation, anomaly detection, and contract enforcement at the point of change altered the economics of failure. Issues surfaced immediately, while scope was small and correction was simple.

Human effort moved upstream. Emergencies disappeared. Response became controlled.[4]

This is the defining characteristic of resilient systems: They fail early and quietly rather than late and loudly.

[FRAMEWORK STEP 2: DEFINE AFTER STATE]

The organization reframed quality as **early detection,** not late correction.

After State Defined (Anonymized)

- Automated validation checks at ingestion and transformation
- Threshold-based anomaly detection on critical metrics
- Schema and contract enforcement
- Alerts triggered at defect introduction, not consumption

Instead of discovering failure through business symptoms, the system surfaced issues **at the point of origin.**

Human effort shifted:

- From emergency response
- To controlled intervention

Failure was not eliminated—but its **impact window collapsed.**

In the after state, failure still occurred—but its impact collapsed.

Because detection happened at the point of origin, fixes were local. Downstream teams remained unaffected. Business cycles continued uninterrupted.

Human judgment became more valuable. Instead of reacting under pressure, engineers intervened deliberately.

This is how systems become robust without becoming rigid. Failure is acknowledged, bounded, and managed—not denied or dramatized.

Quantifying avoided disruption

The value of early detection lies in what never happens.

No all-hands calls. No last-minute reconciliations. No cascading explanations. These avoided disruptions are real, but they must be quantified carefully to remain credible.

By comparing representative late-stage incidents to early-stage intervention, the organization isolates the effort difference attributable to timing alone. No assumptions about defect frequency are embedded here—only response effort per incident.[5]

This conservative framing ensures that the value claimed is defensible and repeatable.

[FRAMEWORK STEPS 6 & 9: EFFORT PER STEP, DELTA CALCULATION]

The value here is **disruption avoided**, quantified conservatively.

Representative Late-Stage Incident (Before)

When a defect escaped detection:

- Incident response involved:
  - 2 data engineers (6 hours each)
  - 1 analyst (4 hours)
  - 1 manager (2 hours)

Total effort per incident:

(2 × 6) + 4 + 2 = 18 hours

Early Detection Effort (After)

- Issue detected automatically
- Single engineer intervention
- ~2 hours to correct upstream

Effort Delta Per Incident

18 – 2 = 16 hours avoided

The effort delta is clear: Fewer people. Less time. No escalation.

What changed was not the existence of defects but the cost of responding to them. Early detection turned multi-team emergencies into single-engineer fixes.[6]

This is the economic core of prevention: not perfection but cheaper failure.

Speed as a form of operational insurance

Speed is often framed as a productivity metric. In operational quality, it is also a risk control.

The faster a defect is detected, the fewer systems consume it. The fewer systems consume it, the smaller the impact. Speed reduces exposure.

By scaling effort avoided across realistic incident frequency and applying a blended rate, the organization translates timing into economic terms—without monetizing trust, reputation, or decision delay.[7]

This restraint matters. It keeps the claim grounded in observable behavior.

Speed here functions as insurance—not because failure disappears but because its consequences are limited.[8]

[FRAMEWORK STEPS 7 & 8: SCALE ACROSS TIME, APPLY RATE]

Frequency Assumption (Explicit)

- Material incidents previously occurring: **12 per year** (roughly monthly)

Annual Effort Avoided

16 hours × 12 incidents = 192 hours/year

Blended Rate Assumption

- Engineering, analytics, and management involvement
- Fully loaded blended rate: **$165/hour**

Direct Annualized Value

192 hours × $165/hour = $31,680 per year

Why This Is Conservative

This calculation excludes:

- Lost trust during incidents
- Delayed decisions
- Reputational impact
- Downstream rework in business teams

It monetizes **only response effort avoided.**

Speed here functions as **operational insurance:**

- The faster a failure is detected,
- The smaller its cost,
- The lower its risk exposure.

The calculated savings represent only avoided response effort. They do not include downstream disruption, lost confidence, or deferred decisions—all of which were reduced materially.

Even within this narrow frame, the value is recurring and durable. Each year, the same early detection prevents the same escalation.

This is how resilience shows up financially—not as dramatic avoidance but as steady reduction in exposure.

The failure-left pattern

Patterns endure when they change posture.

The failure-left pattern shifts organizations from reactive containment to preventative control. By detecting defects at the point of introduction, systems protect the business from feeling their effects.[9]

This pattern applies wherever quality issues propagate silently until they surface as incidents.

Failure-left does not promise fewer mistakes. It promises smaller consequences.

[FRAMEWORK STEP 10: TRANSLATE INTO BUSINESS LANGUAGE]

This example demonstrates a critical enterprise pattern:

When failure is detected early, its cost collapses before the business feels it.

BUSINESS TRANSLATION

This initiative delivered:

- **Lower incident response cost**
- **Reduced cross-team disruption**
- **Higher confidence in operational stability**

More importantly, it changed posture:

- Quality became preventative
- Incidents became contained
- Teams stopped living in reactive mode

This is not perfection.

It is **controlled failure with minimal impact.**

The failure-left pattern changes how organizations experience quality.

Incidents become contained. Response becomes routine. Confidence increases because surprises diminish.

Teams stop living in reactive mode. Quality becomes preventative by design.[10]

This is not perfection.

It is controlled failure with minimal impact.

And with this chapter, the framework reaches its final operational dimension:

- Flow (Chapter 10)
- Decision latency (Chapter 11)
- Awareness (Chapter 12)
- Capacity (Chapter 13)
- Progress (Chapter 14)
- Economics (Chapter 15)
- Complexity reduction (Chapter 16)
- Attention management (Chapter 17)
- Value persistence (Chapter 18)
- Failure containment (Chapter 19)

Same framework.

Different risk surface.

Durable resilience.

Tying it all together

This chapter focuses on a form of value that is easiest to overlook: the cost of problems discovered too late.

To make that cost visible, the following example shows how earlier detection translates into measurable operational savings.

Using a standard value articulation framework, it connects automated quality checks and anomaly detection to reduced disruption and response effort.

The sections are presented exactly as they would be in practice, illustrating how speed becomes a form of operational insurance.

1. TITLE

Reducing Incident Impact Through Early Detection and Automated Validation

2. CURRENT SITUATION

(In business terms, what was the gap or the need?)

Data and operational issues were typically detected only after downstream systems or business processes were affected. While failures were rarely catastrophic at the moment they occurred, they became expensive because they were discovered late.

This created a recurring business gap:

- Firefighting during reporting and planning cycles
- Last-minute corrections involving multiple teams
- Disruption to decision-making and delivery schedules
- Management time consumed coordinating responses

The issue was not the existence of defects. It was the timing of detection.

3. OBJECTIVE

(In business terms, what was the business trying to solve?)

The business objective was to reduce the cost and disruption of operational failures by detecting issues earlier in the data and delivery lifecycle.

Specifically, the organization aimed to:

- Identify defects at the point of introduction rather than consumption
- Reduce the number of people involved in issue resolution
- Shorten the time between detection and correction
- Contain failures before they affected business users

4. SOLUTION

(What was the solution and how did analytics products/services assist?)

Automated validation and anomaly detection were embedded directly into ingestion and transformation workflows.

Key elements of the solution included:

- Rule-based quality checks at data entry points
- Threshold and pattern-based anomaly detection on critical metrics
- Schema and contract enforcement to catch breaking changes
- Alerting triggered by defect introduction, not downstream symptoms

Analytics products enabled issues to be surfaced as technical signals rather than business disruptions.

5. BUSINESS VALUE

(Describe the business value in VERY SPECIFIC terms.)

This initiative significantly reduced the effort required to respond to data-related incidents.

As a result:

- Fewer teams were pulled into reactive investigations
- Issues were corrected earlier and with less coordination
- Reporting cycles experienced fewer last-minute disruptions
- Operational confidence increased as failures became contained events

The value was not perfection. It was smaller, cheaper failures.

6. BUSINESS VALUE CALCULATION DETAILS

(Describe in very specific terms HOW the business value was calculated.)

To quantify value, the organization compared response effort for late-detected incidents versus early-detected issues.

Representative Incident Effort (Before):

- 2 engineers × 5 hours each
- 1 analyst × 4 hours
- 1 manager × 2 hours
- Total effort: ~16 hours per incident

Early Detection Effort (After):

- 1 engineer × ~2 hours

Effort Avoided per Incident:

- 16 – 2 = ~14 hours

Frequency Assumption (Conservative):

- ~10 material incidents per year

Annual Effort Avoided:

- 14 hours × 10 incidents = ~140 hours per year

Blended Fully Loaded Rate:

- Engineering, analytics, and management roles: ~$160/hour

7. TOTAL AMOUNT OF VALUE FOR THE YEAR (IN $)

140 hours × $160/hour = ~$22,400 per year

$22,400 cost avoided in Year 1
$67,200 cost avoided in Year 3

This figure reflects direct labor savings from reduced incident response effort.

It intentionally excludes:

- Lost trust during disruptions
- Delayed decisions and downstream rework
- Reputational or customer impact

Those benefits exist but were not monetized to keep the estimate conservative and defensible.

PART IV

ADVANCED & NON-OBVIOUS VALUE

Part IV exists because the easiest value to quantify is rarely the most important.

Labor savings are the gateway drug: clean math, quick conversions, easy rollups. And sometimes that's the right story. But if you stop there, you'll miss the value that actually changes how the business competes—value that shows up as fewer bad decisions, fewer incidents, faster recovery, better margins, and options the organization didn't have before.

This section is about the value that doesn't photograph well.

We'll start by expanding the lens beyond hours and headcount. You'll learn how to quantify risk reduction without pretending to predict the future—by using exposure, history, near-misses, and plausible impact ranges. We'll tackle prevention, resilience, and the uncomfortable reality that your biggest win may be a negative event that never happens.

Then we'll move into the non-obvious economic categories most teams leave on the table: optionality, flexibility, and avoided downstream costs. The work that collapses future effort. The architecture that turns a six-month integration into a configuration change. The control that prevents a small defect from becoming a multi-quarter remediation program in someone else's budget.

Finally, we'll address credibility. Advanced value fails when it's framed as "intangibles." It succeeds when it's framed as observable before-and-after change with disciplined assumptions—specific enough to be believed, humble enough to survive scrutiny.

This is where quantified impact stops being a labor story.

And becomes a business story.

CHAPTER 21

VALUE BEYOND LABOR SAVINGS

"Customers don't buy products;
they hire them to do a job."

— CLAYTON M. CHRISTENSEN

Why labor is only the starting point

Labor savings are seductive because they're easy to count. You reduce headcount or hours, multiply by a loaded rate, and voilà—a number appears. Finance nods. The spreadsheet balances. Everyone moves on.

But here's what practitioners learn after a few painful conversations: Labor savings are often the least impressive thing your work accomplished. They're just the easiest thing to point to.[1]

Consider what improves even when headcount stays flat: Decision speed. Error rates. Customer experience. Employee frustration. Compliance posture. The ability to say yes to new work without hiring. None of these show up in a headcount reduction, yet each one changes how the business operates.

A team that used to spend three days validating data before a board meeting now spends three hours. No one was fired. But leadership now trusts the numbers—and makes faster calls because of it.

Labor savings also fail when the real value is quality, not speed. Automating a report doesn't just save time; it eliminates transcription errors that once caused pricing mistakes. The hours saved are a footnote compared to the margin preserved.

The trap is this: When you lead with labor, you invite labor-based objections. "We didn't actually reduce headcount." "Those hours just got absorbed elsewhere." "People are still busy." These critiques are valid—if labor is your only claim.

But they fade the moment you shift the conversation to outcomes that matter whether anyone's calendar got lighter.

Labor is a fine starting point. But if it's also your ending point, you've undersold the work before anyone had a chance to understand it.

Risk reduction as measurable value

Risk is one of those words that sounds important until someone asks you to put a number on it. Then it becomes slippery. Uncertain. Easy to dismiss.[2]

But here's the practitioner move: You don't need to predict the future. You need to document the past.

What specific risks existed before the work that no longer exist after? Start there. Maybe it was a manual reconciliation step that failed twice last year, causing a week of fire drills each time. Maybe it was a single point of failure—one person who, if they quit or got sick, would leave the team blind. Maybe it was a compliance gap that hadn't been caught yet but was sitting there like an undetonated mine.

Now ask: How frequently did these risks materialize—or nearly materialize? "Nearly" matters more than most people admit. The close call that didn't become an incident is still evidence of exposure. If you've had three near misses in eighteen months, you're not lucky. You're overdue.[3]

Finally, ask what leadership would have paid to avoid just one occurrence. Not hypothetically—actually. What did the last incident cost in overtime, reputation, executive attention, or delayed projects?

That number exists. Someone knows it, even if it was never written down.

Risk reduction becomes measurable the moment you stop treating it as a vague category and start treating it as an exposed cost that just hasn't hit the P&L yet. Your job is to show the invoice that never arrived—and make clear that its absence wasn't an accident.

Optionality and future flexibility

There's a category of value that doesn't show up in this quarter's results but changes everything about next year's choices. It's called optionality—and most teams give it away for free because they don't know how to price it.

What constraints were removed that expand future decision-making? Maybe you migrated from a rigid legacy system to something modular. Maybe you finally documented tribal knowledge, so the business isn't hostage to one analyst's memory. Maybe you built a data pipeline that can absorb new sources without a six-month integration project.[4]

None of these save money today. But they collapse the cost of future decisions.

Flexibility also changes response time, not just cost. When a competitor moves, when regulations shift, when leadership pivots strategy—how fast can you react? The team stuck on a brittle system needs months. The team with optionality needs weeks. That gap isn't theoretical. It shows up in market timing, customer retention, and the ability to say "yes" while others are still scoping.[5]

The hardest part is articulating what future initiatives become possible only because of this work. You're not predicting. You're describing doors that were previously locked.

"Before this, launching in a new region required a parallel data infrastructure. Now it requires a configuration change." That's not speculation. That's architecture.

Optionality is the compound interest of technical work. It accrues quietly, pays off unexpectedly, and is almost never credited to the people who created it. Change that, and you change how the organization values foundational investment.

Avoided downstream costs

Every decision has a wake. Most of it is invisible until the invoice arrives.

Downstream costs are the expenses that would have appeared later—in another budget, another quarter, another team's problem—if nothing had changed. They're the support tickets from a confusing interface. The rework from bad data that propagated through three systems. The audit finding that triggers a remediation project no one planned for.[6]

The reason downstream costs are so dangerous is that they're diffuse. No single person owns them. They show up as "cost of doing business" scattered across a dozen line items. The team that created the problem is long gone. The team paying for it doesn't know who to blame.

This is also why downstream costs are harder to detect but more expensive. They compound. A small data quality issue in ingestion becomes a reconciliation problem in finance becomes a restatement risk in reporting. Each handoff adds cost and distance from the root cause.[7]

To quantify avoided downstream costs, trace the path forward: What downstream work would have been required if nothing changed? Who would have paid that cost—and when would it have appeared?

Often, the answer is "someone else, later." That's not a reason to ignore it. That's exactly why it gets ignored everywhere else.

When you show leadership the downstream cost you prevented, you're not claiming credit for someone else's savings. You're revealing the full cost of a problem they never knew they almost had.

Secondary and compounding effects

First-order value is what happens immediately. Second-order value is what happens because of what happened. Most teams stop at the first order and leave the rest on the table.

What behaviors changed as a result of the initial improvement? This is where compounding begins. You automated a report, and now an analyst has regained four hours a week. That's first-order.[8]

But what did they do with those hours? If they built a new dashboard that sales now uses to prioritize leads, that's second-order—and it may be worth more than the original automation.

Compounding also scales with volume, time, and adoption. A process improvement that saves 10 minutes per transaction is modest at one hundred transactions a month. At 10,000, it's transformational. Value that looks incremental in a pilot can become strategic at scale—but only if you track the trajectory, not just the snapshot.

A simple test for whether secondary effects are real: Would they disappear if the system reverted? If yes, you've identified dependent value. The new behavior exists only because the underlying capability exists. Remove the foundation, and the structure collapses.

This is why storytelling matters as much as math. Secondary effects require narrative. You have to show the chain: "We did X, which enabled Y, which allowed Z." Each link must be credible.

But when the chain holds, you're no longer presenting a single improvement. You're presenting a system of value that reinforces itself.

That's the difference between a project and a capability.

Presenting non-labor value credibly

The moment you mention "intangible benefits," half the room checks out. Finance hears, "I can't prove this." Leadership hears, "This is feelings, not facts." You've lost before you started.

The fix isn't to avoid non-labor value. It's to present it like evidence, not aspiration.

What evidence makes non-labor value feel real to skeptics? Specificity. Instead of "improved decision-making," say "reduced board-prep time from five days to eight hours, allowing leadership to request ad-hoc analyses they previously wouldn't attempt." Instead of "better collaboration," say "cross-functional teams now share a single source of truth, eliminating the weekly reconciliation meeting that consumed six directors for two hours."[9]

Avoiding speculation doesn't mean avoiding non-labor value. It means anchoring claims in observable changes. What's different now that wasn't before? Who does something they couldn't do? What stopped happening that used to happen?

The framing that turns soft benefits into defensible claims is before-and-after contrast:

Before, X. After, Y. The delta is Z.

You don't need to prove that faster decisions are worth exactly $412,000. You need to show decisions are faster, that speed matters here, and the change is attributable to the work.

The skeptic doesn't need a perfect number. They need confidence the number isn't zero.

CHAPTER 22

SECURITY, RESILIENCE, AND "NEGATIVE EVENTS THAT NEVER HAPPEN"

"Risk comes from not knowing what you're doing."

— WARREN BUFFETT

The challenge of quantifying prevention

Prevention is the hardest value to sell because success looks like nothing: The breach that didn't happen. The outage that was avoided. The compliance finding that never appeared. You're asking people to pay attention to a dog that didn't bark.

Why does prevention feel invisible even when it's working? Because humans are wired to notice events, not non-events. We remember the fire. We forget the smoke detector. Every cognitive bias favors the dramatic over the steady, the crisis over the control.

Leaders discount avoided disasters for the same reason. If the disaster never happened, how do we know it would have? Maybe we got lucky. Maybe the risk was overstated. The counterfactual is always deniable—and denial is easier than gratitude.

Prevention also differs from optimization in storytelling. Optimization has a clear before and after: Slower, then faster. More expensive, then cheaper. Prevention has only "before" and "still fine." The narrative arc is flat. There's no climax, no resolution, no transformation to celebrate. Just continued normalcy.[1]

This is why security and resilience teams struggle to justify investment. They're not delivering features. They're delivering the absence of catastrophe. And absence, no matter how valuable, doesn't photograph well.

The solution isn't to manufacture drama. It's to reframe normalcy as an achievement: Document what was at risk, what was done to address it, and what would have happened without intervention.

Prevention becomes visible only when you describe the disaster that almost was.

Baseline risk and exposure modeling

Before you can claim you reduced risk, you have to prove risk existed. That means building a baseline—a credible picture of what was exposed before controls were added.

What was the realistic exposure? Not the worst-case scenario designed to scare executives but an honest assessment of what was likely, what was possible, and what was already happening in similar organizations. Overstating the baseline destroys credibility. Understating it erases the problem.

Here's what practitioners know: Most organizations rely on luck more than they admit. That manual workaround that "always works?" It works until it doesn't. That spreadsheet with production credentials in column G? It's been fine for three years—until it's not. Luck isn't a control. It's deferred risk.[2]

How often were teams relying on luck instead of design? Document it. Not as judgment, but as observation.

"Before this control, a single misconfigured permission could have exposed customer data. That configuration was managed manually and had been changed 14 times in the past year without formal review."

The assumptions behind your risk model must be stated explicitly. What probability did you assign to incident occurrence? What impact range did you assume? Why?

Credibility lives in the assumptions. A skeptic won't argue with your math. They'll argue with your inputs. Make those inputs defensible—ideally, sourced from internal incident history, vulnerability data, audit results, industry benchmarks, or regulatory guidance—and the model becomes hard to dismiss.[3]

Incident frequency and impact ranges

Predicting exactly when something will go wrong is impossible. Predicting that something will go wrong, eventually, is not. The goal isn't precision. It's bounded uncertainty.

What historical signals suggest likely incident frequency? Start with what's already happened. Near misses count. Audit findings count. Complaints, workarounds, escalations—all of it is signal. If a similar organization had a breach last year, that's not irrelevant trivia. That's evidence of industry-wide exposure.

Impact ranges must be wide enough to be believable but narrow enough to be useful. "Somewhere between $10,000 and $50 million" tells leadership nothing. "Based on similar incidents in our sector, likely impact ranges from $200,000 to $2 million, with tail-risk scenarios exceeding $5 million" gives them something to work with. The range acknowledges uncertainty. The boundaries show you've done the analysis.[4]

Communicating uncertainty without weakening the claim is an art. The trick is to separate what you know from what you're estimating, and to be transparent about which is which.

"We know there were seven near-miss events in the past eighteen months. We estimate that without intervention, the probability of a material incident within 12 months was approximately 30–40%, based on comparable incident rates in peer organizations."

That's not speculation. That's structured reasoning.

Skeptics respect humility more than false confidence. Admit what you don't know, and they'll trust what you do.

Effort avoided during crises

Crises reveal hidden costs that don't exist in normal operations. When something breaks, everyone drops what they're doing. Calendars get cleared. Executives get summoned. Sleep gets sacrificed. The meter runs at a rate that never appears in any project budget.

What manual effort appears only during incidents? Think about who gets pulled in: security analysts, legal, communications, engineering leads, customer support, executives who normally never touch the systems in question. Every one of them has a day job that stops the moment the incident begins. That displacement is a cost—even if it never shows up on an invoice.[5]

Crisis labor also costs more than day-to-day operations. It's unplanned, so it disrupts scheduled work. It's urgent, so it happens at premium rates (overtime, weekends, contractors on emergency retainers). It's high-stakes, so mistakes compound faster and corrections cost more.

Who gets pulled into crisis response—and at what cost? Map it out. Not generically but specifically:

"The last major incident required 48 hours of dedicated time from six senior engineers, plus 12 hours from the CISO, plus external forensics at $450/hour."

Now you have a number. Now you can say: "Reducing incident frequency by one event per year avoids approximately $X in crisis labor alone—before we count customer impact, regulatory exposure, or reputational damage."

Prevention isn't just about avoiding the disaster. It's about avoiding the fire drill that follows.

Translating resilience into dollars

Resilience sounds like a buzzword until you watch costs spike during an outage. Then it becomes the most concrete concept in the room.[6]

What costs spike during outages, breaches, or failures? Revenue loss from downtime. Customer credits or refunds. Emergency contractor fees. Expedited shipping to recover inventory. Legal review for regulatory notification. PR support for damage control. Each of these has a number. Each of these is avoidable—or at least reducible—with the right resilience investment.

Faster recovery changes total financial exposure even when incidents still occur. An organization that recovers in two hours has a fundamentally different risk profile than one that recovers in two days. Same incident. Wildly different cost. Mean Time to Recovery (MTTR) isn't just a technical metric. It's a financial lever.[7]

Which costs are avoided even when incidents still occur? This is the subtler point. Resilience doesn't promise perfection. It promises containment. A well-designed system fails gracefully—affecting one region instead of all of them, one product line instead of the entire catalog, one hour instead of one week. The incident still happens. The disaster doesn't.

Translating resilience into dollars requires you to model both sides: what an uncontained incident would have cost versus what a contained incident actually cost. The difference is the value of resilience. It's not hypothetical. It's the spread between "what happened" and "what would have happened without the investment."

Defending prevention-based value

The moment you claim credit for something that didn't happen, someone will push back. "How do you know it would have happened?" "You're just guessing." "We've never had that problem before." These objections feel reasonable. They're also lazy. Your job is to make them harder to sustain.

What objections do leaders raise against "nothing happened" value? The most common is survivorship bias dressed up as skepticism. "We've been fine so far" ignores the role of luck, ignores near misses, and ignores changing-threat landscapes. Another objection is the counterfactual itself: "You can't prove what would have happened."

This is technically true and practically irrelevant—insurance companies price risk every day without proving specific future events.

Comparative framing strengthens the argument. What happened to similar organizations that didn't invest? What do industry benchmarks show? What does regulatory guidance recommend? If peer companies averaged two incidents per year before adopting similar controls, your prevention claim isn't speculation. It's pattern recognition.[8]

What documentation makes prevention claims audit-safe? Evidence of the pre-existing risk (audit findings, incident logs, vulnerability assessments). Evidence of the intervention (control implementations, configuration changes, process updates). Evidence of post-intervention exposure (new assessments, reduced findings, clean audits).

The trail should show: Risk existed, action was taken, risk decreased.

Prevention value is defensible when you stop arguing about the future and start documenting the past.

CHAPTER 23

WHEN COST AVOIDANCE BEATS REVENUE

"The only place where success comes before work is in the dictionary."

— VIDAL SASSOON

Why finance prefers avoided cost

Revenue projections require faith. Avoided cost requires subtraction.

When someone presents a revenue opportunity, finance has to believe a chain of assumptions: The market will respond, the sales team will execute, competitors won't undercut, timing will hold. Any link can break. Most do. This is why finance discounts revenue projections—often severely—before they ever reach a budget decision.

Avoided cost is different. It's anchored in existing spend. The invoice is already in the system. The contract is already signed. The baseline is already known. When you show finance that a change will prevent a cost from appearing—or reduce one that already exists—you're not asking them to imagine a future. You're showing them math they can verify.[1]

This is also why avoided cost shows up more reliably in budgets. Revenue appears as upside; it might happen. Avoided cost appears as reduction; it will happen. One is a bet. The other is a certainty. Finance builds plans on certainties.

There are also moments when avoidance becomes strategically more important than growth: tight capital environments, post-acquisition integration periods, margin pressure from pricing competition. In these situations, every dollar not spent is a dollar preserved for higher-priority uses. Avoidance isn't retreat. It's reallocation by other means.

Finance doesn't prefer avoided cost because they lack imagination. They prefer it because they've seen too many projections evaporate. Avoidance is the value claim that survives scrutiny.

Reliability vs. speculative upside

There's a reason your savings-account balance feels different from your stock portfolio, even if the numbers are similar. One is stable. The other could evaporate by Tuesday.

Revenue projections are inherently fragile because they depend on external factors outside anyone's control: Markets shift. Customers churn. Competitors surprise. Regulatory changes rewrite assumptions overnight. Even the best forecast is a probability distribution, not a promise.[2]

Avoided cost is more reliable because it depends on internal factors. You control whether you renegotiate a contract. You control whether you consolidate tools. You control whether you automate a process. External shocks can still change the baseline, but the intervention itself is within your sphere.

How does reliability shift leadership confidence? It changes the decision frame. When leaders evaluate a revenue opportunity, they ask, "What's the probability this works?" When they evaluate cost avoidance, they ask, "What's the risk this doesn't work?" The second question has a shorter list of failure modes.

Stability also unlocks better long-term decisions. If leadership trusts that a cost reduction will persist, they can redeploy those dollars into strategic investments with multi-year horizons. If they're not sure the savings will stick, they hedge—holding the money in reserve rather than committing it.

Reliable value compounds. Speculative value gets discounted into irrelevance.

Avoidance in budget planning

The best time to avoid a cost is before it exists. Once it's in the budget, it has defenders. Once it's been spent, it has precedent. But how about before it's approved? It's just a request. And requests can be denied.[3]

How does avoidance change next year's baseline? When you eliminate or reduce a line item before budget finalization, it never becomes part of the normalized expectation. The organization doesn't plan around it. Doesn't staff for it. Doesn't build processes that depend on it. You haven't just saved money this year—you've reset the trajectory.

What decisions become easier when costs don't appear? New investments compete with existing commitments. A dollar not spent on maintenance is a dollar available for growth. A headcount not added for support is a headcount available for product. Avoidance creates fiscal space—the room to say "yes" to something else without increasing total spend.[4]

This is why avoidance is most powerful before spend is approved. After approval, every reduction is a negotiation. Someone has to give something up. Someone has to explain why their budget is shrinking. The politics are heavy.

Before approval, you're just providing better information. The proposal gets revised. The request gets adjusted. No one loses face because nothing was ever committed.

Budget planning isn't just about what to fund. It's about what not to fund. Avoidance gives leadership options they didn't know they had—before the constraints of committed spend close those options forever.

Multi-year avoidance narratives

A single year of avoided cost is nice. Three years changes the ROI math entirely.

How does avoided cost compound across years? If you eliminate a $200,000 annual expense, you haven't saved $200,000. You've saved $200,000 per year for as long as the avoidance persists. Year one: $200K. Year two: $400K cumulative. Year three: $600K.

An investment that cost $300K to implement now shows a 2× return in 18 months and a 3× return in 36. That's not incremental. That's strategic.

But compounding claims require acknowledging decay and erosion risks. Will the baseline increase over time (inflation, volume growth)? Could the avoided cost reappear through a different mechanism (new regulation, new vendor, new requirement)? What would cause the avoidance to expire?[5]

These questions aren't challenges to avoid. They're challenges to address head on.

"Assuming no change in regulatory requirements and continued vendor contract stability, we project sustained avoidance of $X annually through year three, with reassessment recommended at that point."

The danger of multi-year claims is sounding inflated. Finance has heard too many "over three years" framings that stretch modest one-time savings into impressive-sounding totals. The antidote is transparency: show the math, state the assumptions, acknowledge the risks.

If the claim is valid, it survives scrutiny. If it doesn't survive scrutiny, it shouldn't be made.

Common mistakes in avoidance claims

Nothing kills credibility faster than an avoidance claim that falls apart under questioning. And most claims are more fragile than their authors realize.[6]

Where do teams overreach or double count? The most common mistake is claiming avoidance for costs that were never actually planned. "We avoided hiring five people" sounds compelling until finance asks, "Were those positions ever approved?" If the answer is no, you didn't avoid a cost. You avoided a hypothetical.[7]

Another error: claiming full avoidance when the spend was merely delayed. Pushed to next quarter isn't eliminated.

What language immediately triggers finance skepticism? "Potential savings." "Up to." "Could have cost." These phrases signal that the claim isn't grounded—that you're guessing, not measuring. Finance has pattern-matched on this language. The moment they hear it, their skepticism filter activates.

Poor framing also undermines otherwise valid value. Claiming credit for industry trends: "We would have had to buy this anyway, but now we don't" doesn't hold if everyone else also avoided the same cost. Taking ownership of a change that was already happening—with or without your intervention—invites the obvious objection: "This would have happened regardless."

The fix is discipline. Avoidance claims must be specific, verifiable, and attributable. What cost? Says who? Because of what?

The bar for avoidance should be at least as high as the bar for revenue. Probably higher—because finance already trusts avoidance more. Abusing that trust ruins the advantage.

Making avoidance undeniable

The skeptic's objection to every avoidance claim is the same: "Prove it would have happened." You can't travel to an alternate timeline. But you can build a counterfactual so clear that denial feels unreasonable.[8]

What counterfactual makes the avoided cost obvious? Anchoring to documented plans is the strongest approach. If the cost was in a draft budget, a signed contract, a vendor proposal, or an approved project plan, you're not speculating. You're describing what was going to happen, with evidence that already exists.

"The vendor renewal was priced at $180,000. We renegotiated to $120,000. The delta is $60,000, as documented in the signed amendment."

What data anchors the claim in reality? Comparable instances. If similar organizations paid X, and you didn't, the counterfactual has external support. If your own organization paid X last year and Y this year, the comparison is internal—and indisputable. Historical spend is the best friend of the avoidance claim.

How do you show "this would have happened" convincingly? By describing the default path.

"Without intervention, the existing contract would have auto-renewed at the prior rate. Procurement confirmed no renegotiation was planned until we flagged the opportunity. The difference between auto-renewal and actual outcome is $X."

Avoidance becomes undeniable when you show: The cost was real, the trajectory was set, and the intervention changed the outcome.

That's not a story. That's a receipt.

PART V

MAKING THIS REPEATABLE IN YOUR ORGANIZATION

Part V is about durability.

A framework that only shows up during planning cycles isn't a framework. It's a ceremony. The moment work gets busy—and it always does—anything optional disappears. If quantified impact is going to matter in your organization, it has to become automatic. A habit. A reflex. Part of how work is initiated, delivered, reviewed, and funded.

This section shows how to make that happen without turning value into bureaucracy.

We'll start by turning the Quantified Impact Framework™ into daily behavior—small prompts that replace status language with value language, so teams begin asking "What changed?" as naturally as they ask "What's next?" We'll draw the line between lightweight governance and process tax, using guardrails that enable speed instead of gates that slow delivery.

Then we'll embed value where it belongs: at intake, not at closure. Because retroactive justification is where credibility goes to die. When value is clarified early, scope tightens, weak initiatives get filtered, and delivery stays aligned to outcomes instead of artifacts.

Finally, we'll make it practical: your first 90 days. How to choose safe, meaningful use cases. How to build early wins that create pull. How to socialize results with leaders who shape perception. And how to scale from a few examples into a system that doesn't depend on heroics.

The goal isn't one great value story.

It's a repeatable way of working—where impact is visible by default.

CHAPTER 24

TURNING THE FRAMEWORK INTO A HABIT

"Success usually comes to those who are too busy to be looking for it."

— HENRY DAVID THOREAU

Embedding value thinking into daily work

Frameworks don't fail because they're bad. They fail because they're occasional—something you pull out for steering committees and then put back on the shelf.

Where can value questions replace status questions? Every standup, every check-in, every project review is an opportunity. Instead of, "What did you work on?" try, "What value did you create?" Instead of, "Is the project on track?" try, "Is the expected impact still valid?"

These aren't rhetorical upgrades. They're behavioral signals. When leaders ask about value, teams start thinking about value.

What small prompts change how teams plan work? Pre-mortems with an economic angle: "If we deliver this and it creates no value, what would have gone wrong?" Intake questions that force articulation: "What outcome are we expecting, and how will we know we achieved it?" These prompts don't require new systems. They require new habits.[1]

Repetition normalizes economic thinking. The first time someone asks, "What's the dollar impact?" it feels strange. The fifth time, it feels expected. The twentieth time, teams start asking themselves before anyone else has to.

That's the transition from framework to culture.

The goal isn't to turn every conversation into a finance exercise. It's to make value consciousness reflexive—something teams consider without being asked because it's become part of how work is understood.

That shift doesn't happen through training decks. It happens through daily reinforcement. Small questions. Consistent expectations. Relentless repetition.[2]

Lightweight governance vs. bureaucracy

Governance gets a bad name because most of it is heavy. Approval gates. Committee reviews. Documentation requirements that take longer to complete than the work they're documenting. Somewhere along the way, oversight became obstruction.[3]

What governance adds clarity instead of friction? The kind that answers questions before they're asked. Templates that structure thinking without requiring interpretation. Definitions that prevent arguments about what counts. Thresholds that explain when to escalate and when to proceed.

Good governance removes ambiguity. Bad governance creates it.

Where does governance typically go too far? When every decision requires multiple signatures. When the same information is captured in three different systems. When "compliance" means checking boxes instead of improving outcomes.[4]

A reliable warning sign: People spend more time navigating the process than doing the work the process was supposed to improve.

How do guardrails outperform approval gates? Guardrails define boundaries. Inside those boundaries, teams move freely. Approval gates require permission for movement itself.

The difference is whether you're asking, "May I?" or, "Am I within bounds?" The first slows everything down. The second enables speed with accountability.

The test for lightweight governance is simple: Does it help people make better decisions faster? If yes, keep it. If no, cut it.

Governance should be scaffolding, not a cage.

Teaching teams to quantify impact

Most teams avoid quantifying impact because they think it requires finance skills. It doesn't. It requires the willingness to estimate—and the humility to refine.

What skills matter more than math sophistication? The ability to identify what changes. The ability to describe before-and-after states. The ability to connect activity to outcome. None of these require calculus. All of them require clarity.

A team that can say, "This process used to take three days, and now takes three hours" already has the raw material. The multiplication comes later.[5]

How do you lower the intimidation barrier? Start with ranges, not precision. "Somewhere between $10K and $50K" is infinitely more useful than "I don't know." Normalize approximation. Make it clear the goal isn't audit-ready numbers on the first pass. It's numbers that can be tested and refined.

What early mistakes should be encouraged, not punished? Overestimating. Forgetting to account for costs. Missing downstream effects. Confusing effort with impact.

These mistakes are learning opportunities, not failures. The team that makes them—and gets corrected—learns faster than the team that avoids quantification entirely because they're afraid of getting it wrong.

Teaching quantification isn't about creating finance proxies. It's about building muscle memory. The more often teams practice—even imperfectly—the faster they develop intuition for what drives value.[6]

And intuition, once embedded, doesn't need a spreadsheet for every decision.

Review cadences and reinforcement

A framework that's never revisited becomes a framework that's never used. Value claims drift. Assumptions age. What seemed reasonable at project kickoff may be entirely wrong by project close.[7]

Reviews aren't overhead. They're calibration.

How often should value be revisited to stay relevant? It depends on the lifecycle. Fast-moving projects need checkpoints every sprint or iteration. Long-horizon investments need quarterly reviews. The cadence should match the rate of change. If a lot can go wrong between reviews, the reviews are too far apart.

What happens when reviews focus on learning, not policing? Teams share more. They admit when initial estimates were off. They surface surprises before those surprises become crises.

Policing creates defensiveness. Learning creates curiosity.

The best review conversations are the ones where someone says, "We thought X would happen, but Y happened instead—and here's what we learned from the difference."

How do cadences reinforce behavior without fatigue? By being useful, not ritualistic. If the review surfaces information that changes decisions, people value it. If it's a check-the-box exercise that produces no action, people resent it.[8]

Reinforcement doesn't mean adding more meetings. It means making existing touchpoints value-aware. Slip a value question into the weekly sync. Add a value row to the project dashboard.

Make it inescapable without making it burdensome.

Scaling without slowing delivery

Every successful framework faces the same threat: scale. What worked for one team on one project becomes unrecognizable when applied across an organization. The instinct is to standardize everything. That instinct is wrong.

What elements must stay consistent at scale? Definitions. Without shared vocabulary, comparison becomes impossible. "Cost savings" means one thing in IT and another in Operations, and suddenly you're rolling up numbers that shouldn't be added.[9]

Keep the language tight. Keep the categories stable. Keep the thresholds aligned.

What should remain intentionally flexible? The depth of analysis. The documentation format. The tools used to capture and report. These should adapt to context.

A $50K initiative doesn't need the same rigor as a $5M initiative. Forcing equal treatment creates resentment and waste.

How do you avoid turning the framework into ceremony? By keeping it connected to outcomes. The moment the framework exists for its own sake—when people fill in templates because they're required, not because the information is used—the framework has become ritual.[10]

Combat this by continuously asking: What decisions does this enable? What would we do differently if we didn't have this?

If the answer is "nothing," you've got ceremony, not governance.

Signs the habit is working

Culture change is notoriously hard to measure. But when value thinking becomes habit, the signals are unmistakable.

What changes in how teams talk about work? They stop describing activities and start describing outcomes. "We migrated the system" becomes "We migrated the system, which reduced processing time by 40% and eliminated two reconciliation steps costing $X per month."[11]

The framing shifts from what was done to what was achieved.

How do leaders start asking different questions? Instead of, "Is this on track?" they ask, "Is this still worth doing?" Instead of, "When will it be done?" they ask, "When will we see results?"

Questions reveal priorities. When leaders consistently ask about value, they signal that value is what matters.

What behaviors disappear once value thinking sticks? Scope creep without justification—because every addition now requires an impact statement. Projects defended by effort alone—because "we worked really hard" no longer substitutes for "we delivered something worthwhile."[12]

Retroactive justification fades—because value is discussed upfront, not invented at the end.

The ultimate sign is when the framework becomes invisible. Not because it's been abandoned but because it's been absorbed.

Teams don't need to be reminded to quantify impact. They don't need templates for every conversation. Value thinking has become part of how work is done—reflexive, automatic, embedded.

CHAPTER 25

EMBEDDING VALUE INTO DELIVERY, NOT AFTER THE FACT

"All growth depends upon activity. There is no development ... without effort."

— CALVIN COOLIDGE

Value at intake, not at closure

The worst time to ask, "Was this worth it?" is after the money's been spent. By then, the question is academic. The resources are gone. The only remaining task is deciding how to feel about it.

What changes when value is discussed before work starts? Scope gets sharper. Alternatives get considered. Low-impact initiatives get filtered out before they consume capacity. The conversation isn't "How do we do this?" It's "Should we do this—and if so, how much is it worth?"

Early framing prevents low-impact initiatives from entering the pipeline at all. A project that can't articulate expected value at intake won't suddenly discover value at closure. If the sponsor can't explain what changes and for whom, that's not a project with unclear benefits. That's a project that isn't ready.[1]

What intake questions expose weak proposals quickly?

"What decision will this enable that we can't make today?" "Who will do something different because of this, and what will that difference cost or save?" "What happens if we don't do this?"

These questions aren't punitive. They're clarifying. The proposals that survive are stronger. The proposals that don't were going to disappoint anyway.

Intake is the cheapest place to improve portfolio quality. Every weak initiative stopped here preserves capacity for something better. Every weak initiative funded becomes opportunity cost that compounds until delivery.[2]

Role of PMOs and product teams

In too many organizations, PMOs track delivery. Product teams own features. And value belongs to no one. It floats between functions—everyone's responsibility and therefore nobody's.

How can PMOs shift from tracking to enabling value? By making value part of what gets tracked. Instead of measuring milestones alone, measure milestones and expected outcomes. Instead of reporting status, report status and value trajectory.

A PMO that only knows whether a project is on time has half the picture. A PMO that knows whether a project is still worth being on time has the whole thing.[3]

What accountability belongs with product versus delivery? Product should own the value proposition: what outcome we expect and why it matters. Delivery should own execution: how we achieve the outcome efficiently and at what cost.

The boundary isn't always clean. But the principle is. Product says, "This is what we're building and why." Delivery says, "This is how we're building it and what it costs." Both are accountable for the intersection—where investment meets return.[4]

How do shared models reduce friction between roles? When everyone uses the same definitions, estimates, and success criteria, arguments about ownership fade. The model becomes the shared language. Disputes shift from "That's not my responsibility" to "How do we get the number we agreed on?"

PMOs and product teams aren't natural allies. They become allies when they share a target—and when that target is value, not completion.

Analytics, IT, and shared accountability

Analytics builds the dashboards. IT manages the infrastructure. The business makes the decisions. And somewhere in between, value gets lost in translation.

Where do handoffs dilute ownership of value? At every transition. IT delivers a platform and considers the job done. Analytics delivers a report and considers the job done. The business receives both—but neither team owns whether the output changes anything.[5]

Each function optimizes for its own deliverable. The overall outcome has no owner.

How does shared accountability improve outcomes? When multiple functions are measured against the same result, alignment follows. IT doesn't just deliver uptime; IT delivers uptime that enables analytics that enables decisions that produce value. The chain becomes explicit. Each link is accountable to the next.[6]

What structures support collaboration without confusion? Joint value owners. Cross-functional OKRs. Integrated reviews where all contributing teams are present when impact is assessed. These don't merge functions—they connect them.

Each team keeps its expertise. What changes is the expectation that expertise alone isn't enough.

The hardest part of shared accountability is the conversation after a miss. When value falls short, everyone has an excuse. IT blames requirements. Analytics blames data. The business blames tools.

Shared accountability makes those excuses uncomfortable—because the question isn't "Whose fault is it?" It's "What do we do together to fix it?"

Continuous value checkpoints

Projects don't go wrong at the end. They go wrong in the middle—when assumptions collide with reality, and no one notices until it's too late.[7]

What signals indicate value is drifting off course? Scope expansion without corresponding value increase. Cost overruns without reassessing ROI. Stakeholder enthusiasm fading without explanation. Requirements changing in ways that no longer trace back to original objectives.

These aren't always red flags; they're yellow—warnings that the value case may need revisiting.

How early should course correction happen? Earlier than you think. The sunk-cost fallacy strengthens with every dollar spent. Course correction at 20% completion is a pivot. Course correction at 80% completion is a write-off.[8]

The math is the same. The psychology is not.

What checkpoints prevent sunk-cost justification? Reviews that explicitly revisit the original value estimate. Not "How close are we to done?" but "How close are we to the value we projected?"

If expected impact has shrunk while remaining cost has grown, the rational decision may be to stop. Checkpoints that ask this question make stopping possible before stopping becomes embarrassing.

Continuous doesn't mean constant. It means rhythmic—aligned to delivery cadence, automatic rather than crisis-driven. The goal is to catch drift while correction is still cheap.

Preventing retroactive justification

There's a specific kind of creativity that appears only at project close: the art of making disappointing results sound acceptable. Different metrics get emphasized. Qualitative benefits suddenly matter more than quantitative ones. The goalposts shift so subtly that no one notices they've moved.[9]

Why is post-hoc value framing dangerous? Because it corrupts the feedback loop. If every project can be justified after the fact, then no project ever fails. And if no project ever fails, nothing is learned.

The organization loses the ability to distinguish between investments that worked and investments that were reframed to look like they worked.

What incentives encourage honest early estimates? Separating the estimator from the evaluator. Making initial value projections visible and persistent—not buried in a kickoff deck no one ever opens again. Rewarding accuracy over optimism.

The team that estimates conservatively and delivers should be celebrated more than the team that estimates aggressively and explains away the miss.

How does transparency reduce storytelling pressure? When everyone can see the original claim, revisionism becomes risky. The gap between "We said X" and "We delivered Y" is public.

Closing that gap with spin is harder than closing it with performance.

Retroactive justification feels harmless. It's just positive framing, right? But it's corrosive. It teaches teams that outcomes don't matter—only narratives do.

Once that lesson takes hold, value quantification becomes theater.

Value-first delivery pattern

Some teams consistently deliver outcomes that matter. Others consistently deliver outputs that don't. The difference isn't talent. It's orientation.

What behaviors distinguish value-first teams? They start with the outcome, not the solution. They ask, "What are we trying to change?" before "What are we trying to build?" They scope to value, not features—cutting things that don't contribute, even if those things are interesting.[10]

They measure progress by impact metrics, not activity metrics.

How does delivery change when value is explicit? Prioritization gets easier. Trade-offs have a tiebreaker. "Which option creates more value?" isn't philosophical—it's calculable.

The backlog stops being a wish list and starts being a ranked portfolio. Items that don't contribute to value either get killed or pushed behind those that do.

Why does this pattern scale better than heroics? Heroics depend on individuals. Value-first delivery depends on process.

When value thinking is embedded at every stage—intake, planning, execution, review—the system produces good outcomes regardless of who's in the room. That's how quality scales across teams, across projects, across years.

The best teams aren't the ones with the most talented individuals. They're the ones where value is so deeply embedded that it doesn't require exceptional people to create exceptional results.[11]

The pattern does the work.

CHAPTER 26

YOUR FIRST 90 DAYS OF QUANTIFIED IMPACT

"Don't wish it were easier. Wish you were better."

— JIM ROHN

Choosing the right first use cases

First impressions are fragile. Choose poorly, and the framework gets labeled as academic overhead. Choose well, and it earns permission to expand.

What makes a use case both safe and meaningful? "Safe" means low political risk—no one's ego is attached to the outcome, and failure doesn't threaten careers. "Meaningful" means the result actually matters: It changes a decision, funds an investment, or kills something that should have died.[1]

The intersection is narrower than most people expect.

Look for operational improvements with clear baselines and low controversy: Processes that already run, already cost money, and already frustrate people.

Where is the signal-to-noise ratio highest? In work that happens frequently, with measurable inputs and outputs. Transaction processing. Report generation. Data reconciliation. These have numbers attached. They happen often enough to measure improvement quickly. And they're boring enough that no one will accuse you of stepping on strategic territory.[2]

Which wins are visible without being controversial? Efficiency gains in back-office functions. Cost reductions where leadership already wants to spend less. Quality improvements in processes that have caused visible pain.

These wins aren't glamorous. They don't transform the business. But they do something more important early on: They prove the discipline works.

The goal of the first-use case isn't to maximize impact. It's to prove impact can be quantified—and that quantifying it produces results leadership trusts.

You're earning credibility, not spending it.

Starting small without losing credibility

There's a fear that small projects produce small impressions. It's misplaced. Small projects with clear outcomes impress more than large projects with muddled ones.

How do you limit scope without trivializing impact? By framing the initiative correctly. "We're testing a new approach to value quantification" sounds optional—and optional work gets ignored. "We're proving this discipline works before scaling" sounds intentional—and intention earns attention.[3]

What constraints actually strengthen trust? Time-boxes, budget caps, and clearly defined success criteria. When you say, "We'll know if this worked in six weeks," you're making a testable claim.

When the claim proves true, credibility compounds.

Constraints aren't limitations. They're commitments. And commitments that are kept change how people listen to you.

What mistakes do first attempts usually make? Overclaiming value. Underestimating timeline. Choosing a use case with too many confounding variables. And, especially: picking something that requires buy-in from too many stakeholders.

If success depends on five teams cooperating perfectly, attribution will be diluted even if the work succeeds.

Start small not because small is all you're capable of but because small is what earns you the right to go big.[4]

Building early wins

A "win" isn't just a positive number. It's a result that changes behavior. Someone should do something differently because of what you delivered—fund something, stop something, trust something.[5]

What defines a win beyond the math? Adoption. Did anyone actually use the output? Did it inform a real decision? A beautifully quantified analysis that sits unopened in a folder isn't a win. It's wallpaper.

How do early wins create pull instead of push? When leaders see results they didn't have to chase, they start asking for more.

"Can you do the same analysis for this other initiative?" is the moment pull begins.

What evidence converts curiosity into demand? Before-and-after comparisons that are hard to argue with. Testimonials from stakeholders describing decisions that changed. Finance validation confirming the numbers hold up.[6]

The goal is social proof—not just that the framework works, but that credible people believe it works.

Early wins compound. The first success makes the second easier to launch. The second makes the third inevitable.

Miss the first one, and you're back to persuading. Nail it, and momentum does the work for you.

Socializing results with leadership

Timing matters. Format matters. Audience matters. A strong result delivered poorly disappears. A modest result delivered well becomes the foundation for something bigger.

Which leaders shape perception more than authority? The ones others watch. Not always the most senior—but the most respected. The skeptic who, once convinced, becomes your advocate. The informal influencer whose opinion shapes hallway conversations.[7]

Find these leaders early. Win them over first. The rest tend to follow.

What narrative structure accelerates understanding? Problem → action → outcome.

"We had a process costing $X because of Y. We changed Z. The result is now $A instead of $X—a delta of $B."

This structure answers the questions leaders actually care about in the order they care about them.

How do you balance confidence with humility? State what happened factually. Attribute uncertainty honestly. Acknowledge what you don't yet know.[8]

"The measured savings are $150K. We believe an additional $30K–$50K may emerge from secondary effects, but we haven't validated that yet."

Confidence isn't certainty. It's clarity about what you're sure of—and what you're not.

Socializing results isn't about credit. It's about permission. The leaders you convince today are the ones who fund tomorrow's expansion.

Scaling from examples to systems

The first success is a story. The second is a coincidence. The third is the beginning of a pattern. But patterns need infrastructure to become systems.

What patterns must repeat before scaling is justified? Value quantification that works across different types of work—cost reduction and revenue impact, technical projects and process improvements.[9]

If the framework only works for one flavor of initiative, it isn't ready to scale. It's a tactic, not a discipline.

What infrastructure prevents hero dependence? Templates that capture information consistently. Definitions that don't require interpretation. Training that enables teams to quantify without waiting for a central expert.

If scaling means "more of you," you haven't built a system. You've created a bottleneck.

Systems outlast individuals. Processes survive promotions.

How do you preserve rigor while increasing speed? By separating what must be consistent from what can be flexible. Enforce definitions, thresholds, and approval criteria. Let format, depth, and tooling adapt to context.[10]

Teams should move quickly inside guardrails—not slowly through gates.

Scaling isn't a goal. It's a consequence. When early examples work, demand grows. Your job is to meet that demand without diluting quality.

That requires infrastructure built before demand overwhelms you—not assembled after.

Establishing long-term value credibility

Credibility takes years to build and minutes to destroy. The choices you make in the first 90 days set direction. The choices you make over the next 900 determine whether you stay on it.[11]

What behaviors sustain trust over time? Consistency. Delivering what you promise. Updating estimates when evidence changes. Admitting when you're wrong.

The team that revises projections as reality shifts is more credible than the team that defends numbers that are no longer defensible.

Trust comes from honesty, not optimism.

How does consistency outperform brilliance? Brilliance is episodic. Consistency is reliable. Leaders trust the team that delivers accurate value estimates every quarter more than the team that produces one dazzling analysis and then disappears.[12]

You don't need to be the smartest person in the room. You need to be the one people can count on.

What shortcuts permanently damage credibility? Over-claiming. Cherry-picking data. Presenting correlation as causation. Taking credit for organic trends. Each might work once.

The second time, someone notices.

And once the label "unreliable" is applied, it's almost impossible to remove.

The long game is the only game. Credibility compounds quietly. Reputation compounds loudly.

Protect the former, and the latter follows. Sacrifice it for short-term wins, and you'll spend years earning it back.

APPENDIX: TEMPLATES, GUIDES & TOOLS

This section contains the practical quantification frameworks used throughout the book. Each template is designed to help you move from intuition to evidence, from "this feels valuable" to "this is measurable impact." These tools focus on before-and-after clarity, identifying value leakage, cascading annualized impact, classifying deltas, strengthening defensibility, and accelerating results in your first 90 days. Use them to turn conversations into numbers and numbers into credibility.

These pages are meant to be working documents. Print them, annotate them, rebuild them in Excel or Power BI, or adapt them to fit your environment. The goal is not perfection. The goal is clarity. Over time, as your discipline in quantification strengthens, these tools will help you build a track record that is visible, defensible, and repeatable.

Before State / After State Comparison Template

Document observable reality — not aspirations

BEFORE STATE

PROCESS STEPS

1. ____________________________
2. ____________________________
3. ____________________________
4. ____________________________

ACTORS (WHO)

Role: ___________ *Count:* _____

Role: ___________ *Count:* _____

Role: ___________ *Count:* _____

EFFORT PER STEP

Step 1: ____ *hrs* × ____ */wk*

Step 2: ____ *hrs* × ____ */wk*

Step 3: ____ *hrs* × ____ */wk*

Step 4: ____ *hrs* × ____ */wk*

FREQUENCY

Occurrences per week: _______

Weeks per year active: _______

HANDOFFS & REWORK

Handoff points: ______________

Avg rework cycles: ___________

Wait time between: ___________

TOTAL WEEKLY EFFORT

_______ *hours / week*

AFTER STATE

PROCESS STEPS

1. ____________________________
2. ____________________________
3. ____________________________
4. ____________________________

ACTORS (WHO)

Role: ___________ *Count:* _____

Role: ___________ *Count:* _____

Role: ___________ *Count:* _____

EFFORT PER STEP

Step 1: ____ *hrs* × ____ */wk*

Step 2: ____ *hrs* × ____ */wk*

Step 3: ____ *hrs* × ____ */wk*

Step 4: ____ *hrs* × ____ */wk*

FREQUENCY

Occurrences per week: _______

Weeks per year active: _______

HANDOFFS & REWORK

Handoff points: ______________

Avg rework cycles: ___________

Wait time between: ___________

TOTAL WEEKLY EFFORT

_______ *hours / week*

THE DELTA

Weekly Effort Avoided: _______ hrs

Blended Rate Applied: $ _______ /hr

Annualized Value: $ ________

Value Leakage Map

Value isn't destroyed in dramatic failures — it leaks quietly through the cracks

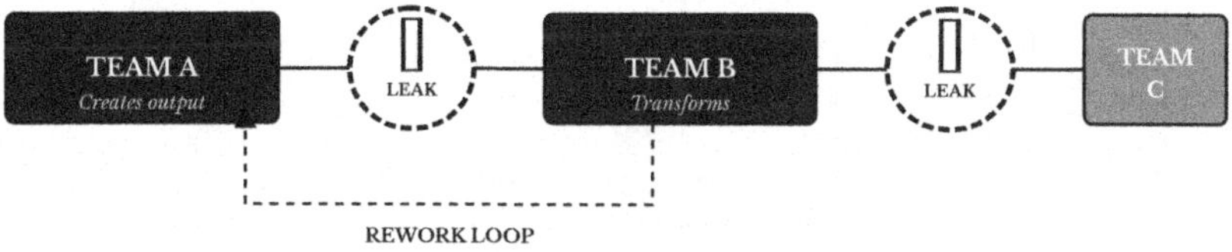

FIVE FRACTURE POINTS

1. HANDOFFS

Every transition between teams introduces delay, interpretation risk, and rework. No one owns the whole outcome — only their slice.

Cost accumulates invisibly because no single team sees the total.

2. REWORK

Requirements change. Context shifts. Outputs technically meet specifications but miss the need. Each iteration consumes time, attention, and credibility — yet rarely gets quantified as loss.

3. COORDINATION OVERHEAD

Meetings to align. Emails to clarify. Calls to confirm. The labor of keeping people synchronized is real work that produces no direct output — but is rarely measured as process cost.

4. WAITING & QUEUE TIME

Work sits idle between steps. Predecessors block successors. Elapsed time grows while labor stays constant. The business moves slower — but no line item captures the delay cost.

5. UNMEASURED EROSION

Value leaks live between org charts. They don't belong cleanly to a function, so they don't appear cleanly in reports. Effort is visible while erosion is not — so erosion wins by default.

Until leaks are translated into economic terms, they are treated as **inconvenience rather than opportunity.**

The Annualization Cascade

Small deltas don't lack value — they lack context

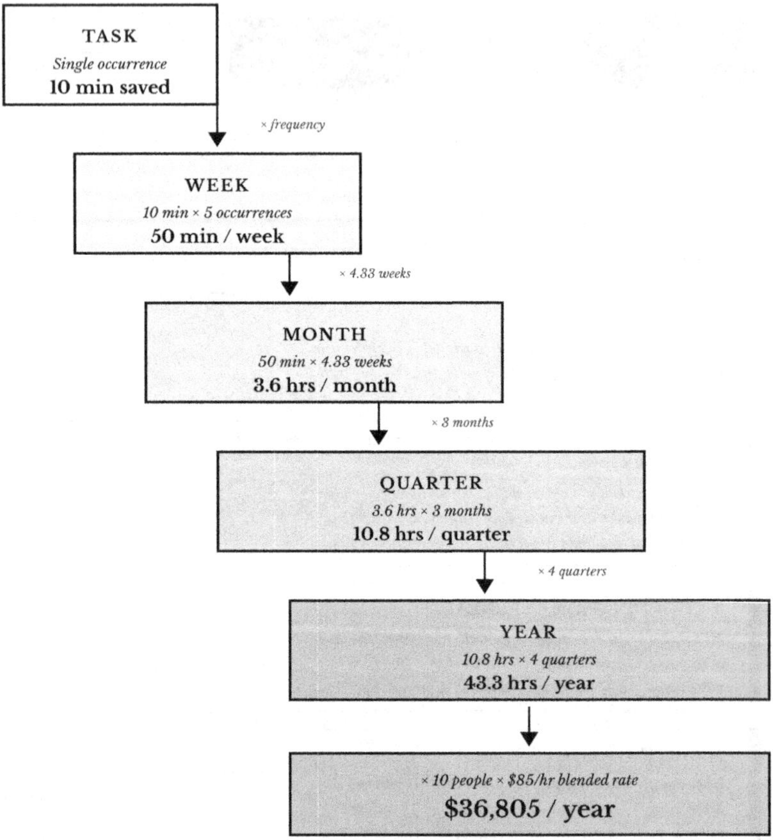

THE COMPOUNDING PRINCIPLE

What the practitioner sees:

"We saved 10 minutes on one task."

Feels trivial.

→

What leadership hears:

"We recovered $36,805 in annual team capacity."

Feels material.

Delta Classification Matrix

Four types of measurable change — know which you're claiming

HOW IT'S MEASURED

WHAT CHANGED	*Labor hours (effort)*	*Elapsed duration (speed)*
Step eliminated	**EFFORT AVOIDED** *The step is gone. No one performs it anymore.* *Highest impact — removes recurring operational burden.* **[] Measure: hrs × rate × 52**	**CYCLE TIME ELIMINATED** *The wait is gone. A dependency no longer exists.* *Unlocks downstream speed and earlier decision-making.* **[] Measure: days removed**
Step still exists	**EFFORT REDUCED** *The step still happens but takes less time or effort.* *Count carefully — the residual effort still counts.* **[] Measure: [] hrs × rate × 52**	**CYCLE TIME COMPRESSED** *The process still spans time but completes faster end-to-end.* *No labor eliminated — but the business moves faster.* **[] Measure: days compressed**

KEY DISTINCTIONS

- **Effort Avoided vs. Effort Reduced**
  "Did the step disappear, or did it shrink?" Avoided removes recurring work entirely. Reduced still incurs residual effort.
- **Time Saved vs. Cycle Time Compressed**
  Time saved = labor (translates to cost via blended rate).
  Cycle time = throughput (translates to speed and responsiveness).
- **Why It Matters**
  Conflating these four categories weakens credibility. Being explicit about which delta you're claiming makes the value easier to defend.

The Defensibility Checklist

Review before every executive conversation

A value claim fails under scrutiny not because the math is wrong — but because the wrong assumptions were treated as important, or the important ones were buried.

I. ASSUMPTIONS

- [ ] ***Does each assumption directly affect the delta?***
  Effort avoided, cost avoided, cycle time, or revenue uplift — if not, remove it.
- [ ] ***Have low-impact assumptions been excluded?***
  Location, tool name, adjacent processes — these invite scrutiny without adding value.
- [ ] ***Can each assumption survive a "so what?" test?***
  Every assumption included invites challenge. Fewer assumptions = harder to dismantle.

II. BEFORE STATE

- [ ] ***Is the before state based on observable behavior?***
  Not aspirations, not assumptions — what people actually did, verified with stakeholders.
- [ ] ***Are process boundaries clearly defined?***
  Where does the process start and end? If boundaries bleed, the delta loses credibility.
- [ ] ***Have handoffs and rework been captured?***
  "Happy path" mapping understates reality. Include coordination, waiting, and iteration.

III. RATES & ROLES

- [ ] ***Do roles map to real job titles in the organization?***
  Invented or abstract roles raise immediate questions. Use recognizable equivalents.
- [ ] ***Do rates reflect how labor is actually sourced?***
  Offshore vs. onshore, FTE vs. contractor — rates must match operating model reality.
- [ ] ***Is the blended rate documented and sourced?***
  Finance will ask. Have the answer ready — with the source, not just the number.

IV. DELTA & SCALING

- [ ] ***Is it clear whether effort was avoided or reduced?***
  "Did the step disappear, or did it shrink?" Conflating the two overstates impact.
- [ ] ***Are monthly and quarterly rollups included?***
  Jumping straight to annual feels speculative. Intermediate steps build trust.
- [ ] ***Would a skeptical CFO find this defensible?***
  The final litmus test. If the answer is no, strengthen the weakest link above.

The First 90 Days of Quantified Impact

You're earning credibility, not spending it.

1

WEEKS 1–2: SELECT & SCOPE

[] *Choose a use case: low political risk, clear baseline*
[] *Look for frequent, measurable work that frustrates people*
[] *Confirm: "Can I explain what changed in one sentence?"*

GATE: Use case identified. Sponsor aligned. Scope defined.

2

WEEKS 3–4: DOCUMENT BEFORE

[] *Map the process: steps, actors, handoffs, rework*
[] *Capture effort per step and frequency*
[] *Validate with practitioners: "Does this match reality?"*

GATE: Before state documented and validated by stakeholders.

3

WEEKS 5–6: DOCUMENT AFTER

[] *Capture the steady-state process (not the transition)*
[] *Separate behavior change from technology change*
[] *Identify: effort avoided vs. effort reduced*

GATE: After state documented. Delta types classified.

4

WEEKS 7–8: CALCULATE & VALIDATE

[] *Apply blended rates. Annualize with intermediate rollups.*
[] *Run the Defensibility Checklist (Figure 6)*
[] *Pressure-test: "Would a skeptical CFO accept this?"*

GATE: Value claim is defensible. Numbers are sourced.

5

WEEKS 9–12: DELIVER & SCALE

[] *Present results in business language to leadership*
[] *Confirm: "Did someone do something different because of what we delivered?" (adoption = the real win)*
[] *Identify the next 2–3 use cases. Begin repeating.*

[]

OUTCOME: Credibility earned. Framework proven. Permission to scale.

The goal of the first use case isn't to maximize impact.
It's to prove impact can be quantified — and that quantifying it produces results leadership trusts.

CITING THE BOOK

APA

Nichol, P. B. (2026). *Quantify Your Impact: How to Turn Everyday Work into Measurable Business Impact* (1st ed.). OROCA Innovations.

CHICAGO

Nichol, Peter B. *Quantify Your Impact: How to Turn Everyday Work into Measurable Business Impact* (1st ed.). Estero, FL USA: OROCA Innovations, 2026.

ELSEVIER HARVARD

Nichol, P 2026, *Quantify Your Impact: How to Turn Everyday Work into Measurable Business Impact*, 1st ed. OROCA Innovations, Florida, USA.

IEEE

P. Nichol, *Quantify Your Impact: How to Turn Everyday Work into Measurable Business Impact*, 1st ed. Estero, FL USA: OROCA Innovations, 2026.

ENDNOTES

PREFACE

1 Kaplan, R.S., & Norton, D.P. (1996).*The Balanced Scorecard: Translating Strategy into Action*. Harvard Business School Press.

2 Porter, M.E. (1987). *Competitive Advantage: Creating and Sustaining Superior Performance*. Free Press.

3 Solow, R.M. (1987). "We'd Better Watch Out," *New York Times Book Review*.

PART I

1 Drucker, P.F. (1967). *The Effective Executive*. Harper & Row.

2 Brynjolfsson, E. (1993). "The Productivity Paradox of Information Technology," *Communications of the ACM* 36, no. 12:66–77.

CHAPTER 1

1 Coase, R.H. (1937). "The Nature of the Firm," *Economica* 4, no. 16: 386–405.

2 Eccles, R.G. (1991). "The Performance Measurement Manifesto," *Harvard Business Review*.

3 DeLone, W.H. & Ephraim, R.M. (2003). "The DeLone and McLean Model of Information Systems Success: A Ten-Year Update," *Journal of Management Information Systems* 19, no. 4:9–30.

4 Varian, H.R. (2019). "Artificial Intelligence, Economics, and Industrial Organization," in *The Economics of Artificial Intelligence: An Agenda*, ed. Ajay Agrawal, Joshua Gans, and Avi Goldfarb. University of Chicago Press.

CHAPTER 2

1 Drucker, P.F. (1973). *Management: Tasks, Responsibilities, Practices*. Harper & Row. (Foundational work on managerial measurement and responsibility.)

2 Kahneman, D. (2011). *Thinking, Fast and Slow.* Farrar, Straus and Giroux.

3 Neely, A. (2002). *Business Performance Measurement: Unifying Theory and Integrating Practice.* Cambridge University Press.

4 Deming, W.E. (1986). *Out of the Crisis.* MIT Press. (Measurement, variation, and process improvement.)

5 McKinsey Global Institute. (2017). *The Power of Automation for Work, Productivity, and Growth.*

6 Davenport, T.H. (1993). *Process Innovation: Reengineering Work through Information Technology.* Harvard Business School Press.

7 Hubbard, D.W. (2014). *How to Measure Anything: Finding the Value of Intangibles in Business.* John Wiley & Sons.

8 Simon, H.A. (1962). "The Architecture of Complexity," *Proceedings of the American Philosophical Society* 106, no. 6: 467–482.

9 Brynjolfsson, E. & McAfee, A, (2014). *The Second Machine Age.* W. W. Norton & Company.

CHAPTER 3

1 Simon, H.A. (1997). *Administrative Behavior.* Free Press.

2 Simon, *Administrative Behavior.*

3 Simon, "The Architecture of Complexity."

4 Hubbard, D.W. (2014). *How to Measure Anything.* John Wiley & Sons.

5 Hubbard, *How to Measure Anything.*

6 Taylor, F.W. (1911). *The Principles of Scientific Management.* Harper & Brothers.

7 Coase, "The Nature of the Firm."

8 Knight, F.H. (1921). *Risk, Uncertainty, and Profit.* Houghton Mifflin.

9 Kahneman, *Thinking, Fast and Slow.*

10 Kahneman, D. & Tversky, A. (1974). "Judgment under Uncertainty: Heuristics and Biases," *Science* 185, no. 4157: 1124–1131.

11 Kaplan and Norton, *The Balanced Scorecard.*

12 Eccles, "The Performance Measurement Manifesto."

CHAPTER 4

1 Kuhn, T.S. (1996). *The Structure of Scientific Revolutions, 3rd ed.* University of Chicago Press.

2 Butterfield, H. (1965). *The Origins of Modern Science.* Free Press.

3 Box, G.P, Hunter, J.S., & Hunter, W.G. (1978). *Statistics for Experimenters.* Wiley.

4 Tufte, E.R. (2001). *The Visual Display of Quantitative Information, 2nd ed.* Graphics Press.

5 March, J.G. (1994). *A Primer on Decision Making: How Decisions Happen.* Free Press.

6 Schwartz, B. (2004). *The Paradox of Choice.* HarperCollins.

7 Johnson, H.T. & Kaplan, R.S. (1987). *Relevance Lost: The Rise and Fall of Management Accounting.* Harvard Business School Press.

8 Mintzberg, H. (1994). *The Rise and Fall of Strategic Planning.* Free Press.

9 Gigerenzer, G. (2014). *Risk Savvy: How to Make Good Decisions.* Viking.

10 Argyris, C. (1993). *Knowledge for Action: A Guide to Overcoming Barriers to Organizational Change.* Jossey-Bass.

11 Ostrom, E. (1990). *Governing the Commons: The Evolution of Institutions for Collective Action.* Cambridge University Press.

CHAPTER 5

1 Rummler, G.A. & Brache, A.P. (1995). *Improving Performance: How to Manage the White Space on the Organization Chart, 2nd ed.* Jossey-Bass.

2 Meadows, D.H. (2008). *Thinking in Systems: A Primer.* Chelsea Green Publishing.

3 Hammer, M. & Champy, J. (1993). *Reengineering the Corporation: A Manifesto for Business Revolution.* HarperBusiness.

4 Harrington, H.J. (1991). *Business Process Improvement: The Breakthrough Strategy for Total Quality, Productivity, and Competitiveness.* McGraw-Hill.

5 Reason, J. (1990). *Human Error.* Cambridge University Press.

6 Dekker, S. (2014). *The Field Guide to Understanding Human Error, 3rd ed.* CRC Press.

7 Tukey, J.W. (1977). *Exploratory Data Analysis.* Addison-Wesley.

8 Taleb, N.N. (2010). *The Black Swan: The Impact of the Highly Improbable, 2nd ed.* Random House.

9 Popper, K.R. (1959). *The Logic of Scientific Discovery.* Routledge.

10 Flyvbjerg, B. (2014). *Survival of the Unfittest: Why the Worst Infrastructure Gets Built—and What We Can Do About It.* Oxford University Press.

CHAPTER 6

1 Lewin, K. (1951). *Field Theory in Social Science.* Harper & Row.

2 Daft, R.L. (2010). *Organization Theory and Design, 10th ed.* South-Western Cengage Learning.

3 Rogers, E.M. (2003). *Diffusion of Innovations, 5th ed.* Free Press.

4 Shirky, C. (2008). *Here Comes Everybody: The Power of Organizing Without Organizations.* Penguin Press.

5 Ohno, T. (1988). *Toyota Production System: Beyond Large-Scale Production.* Productivity Press.

6 Shingo, S. (1989). *A Study of the Toyota Production System.* Productivity Press).

7 Conway, M.E. (1968). "How Do Committees Invent?" *Datamation* 14, no. 4: 28–31.

8 Humble, J. & Farley, D. (2010). *Continuous Delivery.* Addison-Wesley.

9 Perrow, C. (1984). *Normal Accidents: Living with High-Risk Technologies.* Basic Books.

10 Dörner, D. (1996). *The Logic of Failure: Recognizing and Avoiding Error in Complex Situations.* Metropolitan Books.

11 Schön, D.A. (1983). *The Reflective Practitioner: How Professionals Think in Action.* Basic Books.

CHAPTER 7

1 Pande, P.S., Neuman, R.P., & Cavanagh, R.R. (2000). *The Six Sigma Way.* McGraw-Hill.

2 Kotter, J.P. (1996). *Leading Change*. Harvard Business School Press.

3 Little, J.D.C. (1961). "A Proof for the Queuing Formula: $L = \lambda W$," *Operations Research* 9, no. 3: 383–387.

4 Cooper, R. & Kaplan, R.S. (1991). *The Design of Cost Management Systems*. Prentice Hall.

5 Lev, B. (2001). *Intangibles: Management, Measurement, and Reporting*. Brookings Institution Press.

6 Koomey, J.G. (2001). *Turning Numbers into Knowledge: Mastering the Art of Problem Solving*. Analytics Press.

7 Rogers, E.S. & Shoemaker, F.F. (1971). *Communication of Innovations*. Free Press.

8 Savage, S.L. (2009). *The Flaw of Averages*. John Wiley & Sons.

9 Raiffa, H. (1968). *Decision Analysis: Introductory Lectures on Choices under Uncertainty*. Addison-Wesley.

CHAPTER 8

1 Herzberg, F. (1966). *Work and the Nature of Man*. World Publishing Company.

2 Thaler, R. (2015) *Misbehaving: The Making of Behavioral Economics*. W. W. Norton & Company.

3 Chandler Jr,. A.D. (1962). *Strategy and Structure: Chapters in the History of the Industrial Enterprise*. MIT Press.

4 Keynes, J.M. (1936). *The General Theory of Employment, Interest and Money*. Macmillan.

5 Arthur, W.B. (1994). *Increasing Returns and Path Dependence in the Economy*. University of Michigan Press.

6 Romer, P.M (1990). "Endogenous Technological Change," *Journal of Political Economy* 98, no. 5, pt. 2: S71–S102.

7 McGrath, R.G. (2013). *The End of Competitive Advantage*. Harvard Business Review Press.

8 Christensen, C.M. (1997). *The Innovator's Dilemma*. Harvard Business School Press.

9 Marks, H. (2011). *The Most Important Thing*. Columbia University Press.

10 Tetlock, P.E. and Gardner, D. (2015). *Superforecasting: The Art and Science of Prediction*. Crown.

11 Follett, M.P. (1941). *Dynamic Administration*. Harper & Brothers.

CHAPTER 9

1 Box, G.E.P. (2013). *An Accidental Statistician.* John Wiley & Sons.

2 Pearl, J. (2009). *Causality: Models, Reasoning, and Inference, 2nd ed.* Cambridge University Press.

3 Soll, J. (2014). *The Reckoning: Financial Accountability and the Rise and Fall of Nations.* Basic Books.

4 Daston, L. & Galison, P. (2007). *Objectivity.* Zone Books.

5 Hull, J.C. (2015). *Risk Management and Financial Institutions, 4th ed.* John Wiley & Sons.

6 Taleb, N.N. (2012). *Antifragile: Things That Gain from Disorder.* Random House.

7 Power, M. (1997). *The Audit Society: Rituals of Verification.* Oxford University Press.

8 Deming, W.E. (1993). *The New Economics for Industry, Government, Education.* MIT Press.

9 Janis, I.L. (1982). *Groupthink, 2nd ed.* Houghton Mifflin.

10 Duarte, N. (2010). *Resonate: Present Visual Stories That Transform Audiences.* John Wiley & Sons.

CHAPTER 10

1 Beer, S. (1981). *Brain of the Firm, 2nd ed.* John Wiley & Sons.

2 Forrester, J.W. (1961). *Industrial Dynamics.* MIT Press.

3 Bowersox, D.J., Closs, D.J., & Cooper, M.D. (2010). *Supply Chain Logistics Management, 3rd ed.* McGraw-Hill.

4 Johnson, H.T. (2000). *Profit Beyond Measure: Extraordinary Results through Attention to Work and People.* Harvard Business School Press.

5 Teece, D.J. (2009). *Dynamic Capabilities and Strategic Management.* Oxford University Press.

6 Williamson, O.E. (1985). *The Economic Institutions of Capitalism.* Free Press.

7 Nonaka, I. & Takeuchi, H. (1995). *The Knowledge-Creating Company.* Oxford University Press.

8 Parker, G., Van Alstyne, M., & Choudary, S.P. (2016). *Platform Revolution.* W. W. Norton & Company.

CHAPTER 11

1 Simon, H.A. (1996). *The Sciences of the Artificial, 3rd ed.* (MIT Press.

2 Klein, G. (1998). *Sources of Power: How People Make Decisions.* MIT Press.

3 Zuboff, S. (1988). *In the Age of the Smart Machine.* Basic Books.

4 Bar-Yam, Y. (2004). *Making Things Work: Solving Complex Problems in a Complex World.* NECSI Press.

5 Checkland, P. (1981). *Systems Thinking, Systems Practice.* John Wiley & Sons.

6 Fogg, B.J. (2019). *Tiny Habits: The Small Changes That Change Everything.* Houghton Mifflin Harcourt.

7 Thaler, R.H. & Sunstein, C.R. (2009). *Nudge, rev. ed.* Penguin Books.

8 Beer, S. (1974). *Designing Freedom.* CBC Publications.

9 Nightingale, D.J. & Rhodes, D.H. (2008). *Architecting the Future Enterprise.* MIT Press.

CHAPTER 12

1 Lee, H.L. (2004). "The Triple-A Supply Chain," *Harvard Business Review.*

2 Christopher, M. & Peck, H. (2004). "Building the Resilient Supply Chain," *International Journal of Logistics Management* 15, no. 2: 1–14.

3 Slack, N., Chambers, S., & Johnston, R. (2010). *Operations Management, 7th ed.* Pearson Education.

4 Fredrickson, D. & Mitchell, J.L. (2014). *Information Systems and Supply Chain Visibility.* Springer.

5 Westerman, G., Bonnet, D., & McAfee, A. (2014) *Leading Digital.* Harvard Business Review Press.

6 Ashton, K. (2009). "That 'Internet of Things' Thing," *RFID Journal.*

7 Westerman, Bonnet, and McAfee, *Leading Digital.*

8 Sheffi, Y. (2005). *The Resilient Enterprise: Overcoming Vulnerability for Competitive Advantage.* MIT Press.

9 Simchi-Levi, D., Kaminsky, P., & Simchi-Levi, E. (2008). *Designing and Managing the Supply Chain, 3rd ed.* McGraw-Hill.

10 Gawer, A. & Cusumano, M.A. (2002). *Platform Leadership.* Harvard Business School Press.

11 Barratt, M. & Adegoke, O. (2007). "Supply Chain Visibility: A Complex Systems Perspective," *Journal of Business Logistics* 28, no. 1: 121–145.

CHAPTER 13

1 Flyvbjerg, B. (2023). *How Big Things Get Done.* Currency.

2 Kim, G., Humble, J., & Debois, P. (2016). *The DevOps Handbook.* IT Revolution Press.

3 Reinertsen, D. (2009). *The Principles of Product Development Flow.* Celeritas Publishing.

4 Shaw, M. & Garlan, D. (1996). *Software Architecture: Perspectives on an Emerging Discipline.* Prentice Hall.

5 Agrawal, A., Gans, J., & Goldfarb, A. (2018). *Prediction Machines.* Harvard Business School Press.

6 Brynjolfsson, E., Rock, D., & Syverson, C. (2021). "Artificial Intelligence and the Modern Productivity Paradox," *Journal of Economic Perspectives* 35, no. 4: 1–26.

7 Eisenhardt, K. & Sull, D. (2001). "Strategy as Simple Rules," *Harvard Business Review.*

8 McAfee A. & Brynjolfsson, E. (2017). *Machine, Platform, Crowd.* W. W. Norton & Company.

9 Teece, D.J. (2018). "Business Models and Dynamic Capabilities," *Long Range Planning* 51, no. 1: 40–49.

10 Alexander, C. (1977). *A Pattern Language.* Oxford University Press.

CHAPTER 14

1 Brooks Jr., F.P. (1995). *The Mythical Man-Month: Essays on Software Engineering, Anniversary ed.* Addison-Wesley.

2 Hellerstein, J.M., Stonebraker, M., & Hamilton, J. (2007). "Architecture of a Database System," *Foundations and Trends in Databases* 1, no. 2: 141–259.

3 Kleppmann, M. (2017). *Designing Data-Intensive Applications* O'Reilly Media.

4 Parnas, D.L. (1972). "On the Criteria to Be Used in Decomposing Systems into Modules," *Communications of the ACM* 15, no. 12: 1053–1058.

5 D'Aveni, R.A. (1994). *Hypercompetition*. Free Press.

6 Spear, S.J. (2009). *The High-Velocity Edge*. McGraw-Hill.

7 Arthur, B. (1989). "Competing Technologies, Increasing Returns, and Lock-In by Historical Events," *Economic Journal* 99, no. 394: 116–131.

8 West, G. (2017). *Scale: The Universal Laws of Growth, Innovation, Sustainability, and the Pace of Life in Organisms, Cities, Economies, and Companies*. Penguin Press.

9 Wardley, S. (2017). *Wardley Maps: Topographical Intelligence in Business*. Wardley Maps Ltd.

10 Booch, G. (2007). *Object-Oriented Analysis and Design with Applications, 3rd ed.* Addison-Wesley.

CHAPTER 15

1 Davenport, T.H. & Ronanki, R. (2018). "Artificial Intelligence for the Real World," *Harvard Business Review.*

2 Storment, J.R. & Fuller, M. (2020). *Cloud FinOps: Collaborative, Real-Time Cloud Financial Management*. O'Reilly Media.

3 Raynor, M.E. (2007). *The Strategy Paradox*. Currency/Doubleday.

4 Cooper, R. (1995). *When Lean Enterprises Collide: Competing through Confrontation*. Harvard Business School Press.

5 Sterman, J. (2000). *Business Dynamics: Systems Thinking and Modeling for a Complex World.* Irwin/McGraw-Hill.

6 McAfee, A. (2019). *More from Less: The Surprising Story of How We Learned to Prosper Using Fewer Resources*. Scribner.

7 Rappaport, A. (1986). *Creating Shareholder Value*. Free Press.

8 Thaler, R. (1992). *The Winner's Curse: Paradoxes and Anomalies of Economic Life*. Princeton University Press.

9 Ries, E. (2011). *The Lean Startup*. Crown Business.

10 Ton, Z. (2014). *The Good Jobs Strategy*. Houghton Mifflin Harcourt.

11 Andreessen, M. (2011). "Why Software Is Eating the World," *Wall Street Journal.*

12 Ross, J.W., Beath, C.M., & Mocker, M. *Designed for Digital: How to Architect Your Business for Sustained Success*. MIT Press.

CHAPTER 16

1 Lientz, B.P. & Swanson, E.B. (1980). *Software Maintenance Management: A Study of the Maintenance of Computer Application Software in 487 Data Processing Organizations*. Addison-Wesley.

2 Jones, C. (2007). *Estimating Software Costs, 2nd ed.* McGraw-Hill.

3 Kahneman, D., Knetsch, J.L., & Thaler, R.H. "Anomalies: The Endowment Effect, Loss Aversion, and Status Quo Bias," *Journal of Economic Perspectives* 5, no. 1: 193–206.

4 Alderfer, C. (1980). *Explanations of Change in Organizations.* Cornell University Press.

5 Humble, J., Molesky, J., and O'Reilly, B. (2014). *Lean Enterprise.* O'Reilly Media.

6 Nygard, M.T. (2007). *Release It! Design and Deploy Production-Ready Software*. Pragmatic Bookshelf.

7 Markowitz, H.M. (1959). *Portfolio Selection: Efficient Diversification of Investments*. Yale University Press.

8 Gigerenzer, G. (2007). *Gut Feelings: The Intelligence of the Unconscious*. Viking.

9 Cunningham, W. (1992). "The WyCash Portfolio Management System," *OOPSLA '92 Proceedings*.

10 Martin, R.C. (2017). *Clean Architecture: A Craftsman's Guide to Software Structure and Design*. Prentice Hall.

CHAPTER 17

1 Kostoff, R.N. & Schaller, R.R. (2001). "Science and Technology Roadmaps," *IEEE Transactions on Engineering Management* 48, no. 2: 132–143.

2 Lencioni, P. (2002). *The Five Dysfunctions of a Team.* Jossey-Bass.

3 Tyler, T.R. (2006). *Why People Obey the Law.* Princeton University Press.

4 Lessig, L. (2006). *Code: And Other Laws of Cyberspace, Version 2.0*. Basic Books.

5 Szabo, N. (1997). "Formalizing and Securing Relationships on Public Networks," *First Monday* 2, no. 9.

6 Weick, K.E. & Sutcliffe, K.M. (2007). *Managing the Unexpected, 2nd ed.* Jossey-Bass.

7 Hollnagel, E. (2014). *Safety-I and Safety-II: The Past and Future of Safety Management*. Ashgate,.
8 Benkler, Y. (2006). *The Wealth of Networks*. Yale University Press.
9 Hood, C. (1998). *The Art of the State: Culture, Rhetoric, and Public Management*. Oxford University Press.
10 Snowden, D. and Boone, M. (2007). "A Leader's Framework for Decision Making," *Harvard Business Review*.

CHAPTER 18

1 Simon, H.A. (1971). "Designing Organizations for an Information-Rich World," in *Computers, Communications, and the Public Interest*, ed. Martin Greenberger. Johns Hopkins Press.
2 Johnson, C. (2012). *The Information Diet*. O'Reilly Media.
3 Leavitt, H.J. (1965). "Applied Organizational Change in Industry," in *Handbook of Organizations*, ed. James G. March. Rand McNally.
4 Crawford, M. (2009). *Shop Class as Soulcraft*. Penguin Press.
5 Taleb, N.N. (2005). *Fooled by Randomness, 2nd ed*. Random House.
6 Gall, J. (1975). *Systemantics: How Systems Really Work and How They Fail*. Pocket Books.
7 Klotz, L. (2021). *Subtract: The Untapped Science of Less*. Flatiron Books.
8 Rams, D. (2020). *As Little Design as Possible*. Phaidon Press.
9 Wegner, D.M. (2002). *The Illusion of Conscious Will*. MIT Press.
10 Gigerenzer, G. (2002). *Calculated Risks: How to Know When Numbers Deceive You*. Simon & Schuster.
11 Shannon, C.E. (1948). "A Mathematical Theory of Communication," *Bell System Technical Journal* 27, no. 3: 379–423.

CHAPTER 19

1 Flyvbjerg, B., Budzier, A., and Lovallo, D. (2014). "Why Your IT Project May Be Riskier Than You Think," *Harvard Business Review*.
2 Kerzner, H. (2013). *Project Management: A Systems Approach to Planning, Scheduling, and Controlling, 11th ed*. John Wiley & Sons.

3 Aaker, D.A. (2014). *Strategic Market Management, 10th ed.* John Wiley & Sons.
4 Kay, J. (1993). *Foundations of Corporate Success.* Oxford University Press.
5 Gamma, E., Helm, R., Johnson, R., & Vlissides, J. (1994). *Design Patterns: Elements of Reusable Object-Oriented Software.* Addison-Wesley.
6 Sprague Jr., R.H. (1980). "A Framework for the Development of Decision Support Systems," *MIS Quarterly* 4, no. 4: 1–26.
7 Stern, N. (2007). *The Economics of Climate Change: The Stern Review.* Cambridge University Press.
8 Weick, K.E. (1995). *Sensemaking in Organizations.* Sage Publications.
9 Brand, S. (1994). *How Buildings Learn: What Happens After They're Built.* Viking.
10 Kelly, K. (2010). *What Technology Wants.* Viking.

CHAPTER 20

1 Boehm, B.W. & Basili, V.R. (2001). "Software Defect Reduction Top 10 List," *Computer* 34, no. 1: 135–137.
2 Grove, A. (1996). *Only the Paranoid Survive.* Currency Doubleday.
3 Vaughan, D. (1996). *The Challenger Launch Decision.* University of Chicago Press.
4 Burgess, M. (2015). *In Search of Certainty.* O'Reilly Media.
5 Kunreuther, H. & Michel-Kerjan, E.O. (2009). *At War with the Weather.* MIT Press.
6 Slovic, P. (2000). *The Perception of Risk.* Earthscan.
7 Spear, S.M. & Bowen, H.K. (1999). "Decoding the DNA of the Toyota Production System," *Harvard Business Review.*
8 Eisenhardt, K. (1989). "Making Fast Strategic Decisions in High-Velocity Environments," *Academy of Management Journal* 32, no. 3: 543–576.
9 Allspaw, J. & Hammond, P. (2009). "10+ Deploys per Day: Dev and Ops Cooperation at Flickr," Velocity Conference Proceedings.
10 Dekker, S. (2011) *Drift into Failure.* Ashgate.

CHAPTER 21

1 Lindert, P.H. (2004). *Growing Public: Social Spending and Economic Growth since the Eighteenth Century.* Cambridge University Press.

2 Kunreuther, H., Pauly, M., & McMorrow, S. (2013). *Insurance and Behavioral Economics.* Cambridge University Press.

3 Sunstein, C.R. (2002). *Risk and Reason: Safety, Law, and the Environment.* Cambridge University Press.

4 Taleb, N.N. (1997). *Dynamic Hedging.* John Wiley & Sons.

5 Mandelbrot, B. & Hudson, R.L. (2004). *The (Mis)Behavior of Markets.* Basic Books.

6 Cohan, P.S. (2006). *Value Creation: The Power of Brand.* Wiley.

7 Kaplan, R.S. & Norton, D.P. *Strategy-Focused Organization.* Harvard Business School Press.

8 Romer, P. (1986). "Increasing Returns and Long-Run Growth," *Journal of Political Economy* 94, no. 5: 1002–1037.

9 Eccles, R.G., Newquist, S.C., & Schatz, R. (2007). *Reputation and Its Risks.* Harvard Business School Press.

CHAPTER 22

1 Wildavsky, A. (1988). *Searching for Safety.* Transaction Publishers.

2 Kaplan, R.S. & Mikes, A. (2012). "Managing Risks: A New Framework," *Harvard Business Review.*

3 Aven, T. (2015). *Risk Analysis, 2nd ed.* John Wiley & Sons.

4 Kletz, T. (2009). *What Went Wrong? Case Histories of Process Plant Disasters, 5th ed.* Butterworth-Heinemann.

5 Weick, K.E. (1993). "The Collapse of Sensemaking in Organizations," *Administrative Science Quarterly* 38, no. 4: 628–652.

6 Sheffi, Y. & Rice Jr., J.B. (2005). "A Supply Chain View of the Resilient Enterprise," *MIT Sloan Management Review* 47, no. 1: 41–48.

7 Zolli, A. & Healy, A.M. (2012). *Resilience: Why Things Bounce Back.* Free Press.

8 Kahneman, *Thinking, Fast and Slow.*

CHAPTER 23

1 Vance, D. (2003). *Financial Analysis and Decision Making: Tools and Techniques to Solve Financial Problems and Make Effective Business Decisions*. McGraw-Hill.

2 Marks, H. (2013). *The Most Important Thing Illuminated.* Columbia University Press.

3 Rabin, J. (2015). *Budgeting and Financial Management in the Public Sector*. CRC Press.

4 Welsch, G.A., Hilton, R.W., & Gordon, P.N. (1988). *Budgeting: Profit Planning and Control, 5th ed.* Prentice Hall.

5 Cunningham, L.A. (2015). *The Essays of Warren Buffett: Lessons for Corporate America, 4th ed.* Carolina Academic Press.

6 Tetlock and Gardner, *Superforecasting.*

7 Kahneman D.N. & Lovallo, D. (1993). "Timid Choices and Bold Forecasts," *Management Science* 39, no. 1: 17–31.

8 Brealey, R., Myers, S., & Allen, F. (2017) *Principles of Corporate Finance, 12th ed.* McGraw-Hill Education.

CHAPTER 24

1 Duhigg, C. (2012). *The Power of Habit: Why We Do What We Do in Life and Business*. Random House.

2 Amabile, T. & Kramer, S. (2011). *The Progress Principle*. Harvard Business Review Press.

3 Hamel, G. (2012). *What Matters Now: How to Win in a World of Relentless Change*. Jossey-Bass.

4 Brunsson, N. (2002) *The Organization of Hypocrisy: Talk, Decisions, and Actions in Organizations*. John Wiley & Sons.

5 Kolb, D. (2015). *Experiential Learning: Experience as the Source of Learning and Development, 2nd ed.* Pearson Education.

6 Wenger, E. (1998). *Communities of Practice: Learning, Meaning, and Identity*. Cambridge University Press.

7 McChesney, C., Covey, S., & Huling, J. (2012). *The 4 Disciplines of Execution*. Free Press.

8 Edmondson, A.C. (2018). *The Fearless Organization*. John Wiley & Sons.

9 Porter, M.E. & Kramer, M.R. (2011). *Creating Shared Value*. Harvard Business School Publishing.

10 Moore, G. (2015). *Zone to Win*. HarperBusiness.

11 Blau, P.M. (1964). *Exchange and Power in Social Life*. John Wiley & Sons.
12 Hagen, E.E. (1962). *On the Theory of Social Change*. Dorsey Press.

CHAPTER 25

1 Martin, R.L. (2013). *Playing to Win: How Strategy Really Works*. Harvard Business Review Press.
2 Terwiesch, C. & Ulrich, K.T. (2009). *Innovation Tournaments: Creating and Selecting Exceptional Opportunities*. Harvard Business School Press.
3 Turner, R. (2009). *The Handbook of Project-Based Management, 3rd ed*. McGraw-Hill.
4 Cagan, M. (2018). *Inspired: How to Create Tech Products Customers Love, rev. ed*. John Wiley & Sons.
5 Ross, J.W., Weill, P., & Robertson, D.C. (2006). *Enterprise Architecture as Strategy*. Harvard Business School Press.
6 Applegate, L.M., Austin, R.D., & McFarlan, W.R. (2009) *Corporate Information Strategy and Management*, McGraw-Hill/Irwin.
7 Deming, *Out of the Crisis*.
8 Spear and Bowen, "Decoding the DNA of the Toyota Production System."
9 Lovallo, D. & Sibony, O. (2010). "The Case for Behavioral Strategy," *McKinsey Quarterly*.
10 Kotter, J.P. (2014). *Accelerate: Building Strategic Agility for a Faster-Moving World*. Harvard Business School Press.
11 Eisenhardt, K.M. & Sull, D.N. (2015). *Simple Rules: How to Thrive in a Complex World*. Houghton Mifflin Harcourt.

CHAPTER 26

1 Rumelt, R. (2011). *Good Strategy/Bad Strategy: The Difference and Why It Matters*. Crown Business.
2 MacMillan, I.C. & McGrath, R.G. (2009). *Discovery-Driven Growth*. Harvard Business School Press.
3 Rogers, E.M. (2003). *Diffusion of Innovations, 5th ed*. Free Press.
4 Weick, K.E. (1984). *Small Wins: Redefining the Scale of Social Problems, American Psychologist* 39, no. 1: 40–49.
5 Amabile, T. (1996). *Creativity in Context*. Westview Press.

6 Kanter, R.M. (2004). *Confidence: How Winning Streaks and Losing Streaks Begin and End.* Crown Business.

7 Kotter, J.P. & Cohen, D.S. (2002). *The Heart of Change*. Harvard Business School Press.

8 Reynolds, G. (2008). *Presentation Zen.* New Riders.

9 Adler, P.R. & Borys, B. (1996). "Two Types of Bureaucracy: Enabling and Coercive," *Administrative Science Quarterly* 41, no. 1: 61–89.

10 Wilson, J.Q. (1989). *Bureaucracy: What Government Agencies Do and Why They Do It.* Basic Books.

11 Max Weber, M. (1978). *Economy and Society*, ed. Guenther Roth and Claus Wittich. University of California Press.

12 Hart O. & Holmström, B. (1984). "The Theory of Contracts," *Econometrica* 52, no. 2: 247–273.

INDEX

From OROCA Innovations: Author Peter B. Nichol, a 8x author, certified Master Business Relationship Manager (MBRM®) by the BRM Institute and a MIT Sloan School of Management-recognized CIO has finally captured how the most innovative leaders connect strategy to execution—in his most recent book entitled, *Think Lead Disrupt!*

"*Think Lead Disrupt* is a fantastic book for leaders that want to develop innovative ideas that can be translated into world-class business products, services, and interactions. Nichol's voice as a CIO and global thought leader is simple to understand and easy to apply. This is a must read for innova-tors leading teams, departments, or organizations that must be on the cutting edge!"

AARON S. BARNES

CEO AND CO-FOUNDER, BUSINESS RELATIONSHIP MANAGEMENT (BRM) INSTITUTE

Peter B. Nichol—8x author, Master Business Relationship Manager (MBRM®), and MIT Sloan–recognized CIO—writes *Deliver Real Value* for BRMs and role-adjacent professionals positioned between strategy and delivery, rarely empowered to shape either. This book defines disciplined execution inside real organizations and exposes what keeps capable practitioners coordinating instead of influencing outcomes.

"I've seen capable BRMs plateau — not because they lacked talent, but because their role was never clearly defined. *Deliver Real Value* addresses that directly. What I appreciate is the emphasis on disciplined behavior tied to measurable outcomes. This *Deliver Real Value* gives practitioners a way to operate that earns authority through results, not proximity — and that distinction matters at the executive level."

VAUGHAN MERLYN

CO-FOUNDER, BUSINESS RELATIONSHIP MANAGERMENT INSTITUTE

From OROCA Innovations: Author Peter B. Nichol, the first globally certified Masters Business Relationship Management (MBRM®) by the BRM Institute, 8x author, and an MIT Sloan School of Management-recognized CIO and award-winning innovation leader, is your guide to effectively communicate business value with *Leading with Value*.

"Learn how to speak the language of business value! *Leading with Value* is the solution that every business relationship partner has been looking for—the complete guide to effectively communicating business value!"

GLENN REMORERAS,
CHIEF INFORMATION OFFICER, MARK ANTHONY GROUP

From OROCA Innovations: Author Peter B. Nichol, a 8x author, certified Master Business Relationship Manager (MBRM®) by the BRM Institute and a MIT Sloan School of Management-recognized CIO has finally captured how the most innovative leaders connect strategy to execution—in his most recent book entitled, *Think Lead Disrupt!*

"*Think Lead Disrupt* is a fantastic book for leaders that want to develop innovative ideas that can be translated into world-class business products, services, and interactions. Nichol's voice as a CIO and global thought leader is simple to understand and easy to apply. This is a must read for innova-tors leading teams, departments, or organizations that must be on the cutting edge!"

AARON S. BARNES

CEO AND CO-FOUNDER, BUSINESS RELATIONSHIP MANAGEMENT (BRM) INSTITUTE

From OROCA Innovations: Author Peter B. Nichol, an MIT Sloan School of Management-recognized CIO and award-winning innovation leader, explores the for-gotten world of learning—the ability to learn—in the book entitled, *Learning Intelligence.*

"Peter dives into unexplored, valuable territory in *Learning Intelligence.* A must-read for any leader wanting to compete in the innovation-powered landscape of today."

MARSHALL GOLDSMITH,
THE AUTHOR OF THE #1 *NEW YORK TIMES* BESTSELLER, *TRIGGERS*

Recently from OROCA Innovations: Author Peter B. Nichol, an MIT Sloan School of Management-recognized CIO and award-winning innovation leader, explores how blockchain transform the patient experience—in the book entitled, *The Power of Blockchain for Healthcare.*

"*The Power of Blockchain for Healthcare* provides a compelling argument for the transformative impact that blockchain will have on the patience experience. Nichol Magnificently articulates a future vision of health, a vision every executive should experience."

SAN BANERJEE

HEAD OF CONSUMER DIGITAL SOLUTIONS, HUMANA

Peter B. Nichol—8x author and innovation leader—presents *Stay Strong After 60*, a practical guide to improving balance, preventing falls, and maintaining independence as we age. This book explains what happens to strength, coordination, and stability over time—and provides simple, effective exercises to protect mobility, confidence, and an active lifestyle!

"After more than 30 years of golfing, I started losing distance and feeling stiff after 18 holes. *Stay Strong After 60* explained what was happening in my hips, back, and shoulders and showed me how to build the strength I needed to keep playing strong."

ROBERT "BOB" JENKINS,
ACTIVE GOLFER
SCOTTSSDALE, AZ

Made in United States
North Haven, CT
04 November 2026

21766799R00176